Hidden Chains

The Unseen Evil, Volume 2

Natashia Roberts

Published by Natashia Roberts, 2024.

HIDDEN CHAINS

First edition. September 24, 2024.

Copyright © 2024 Natashia Roberts.

ISBN: 979-8227349675

Written by Natashia Roberts.

Table of Contents

Dedicated to all the survivors of this horrific deeds.

To the little ones who didn't survive, and the families forever grieving their loss.

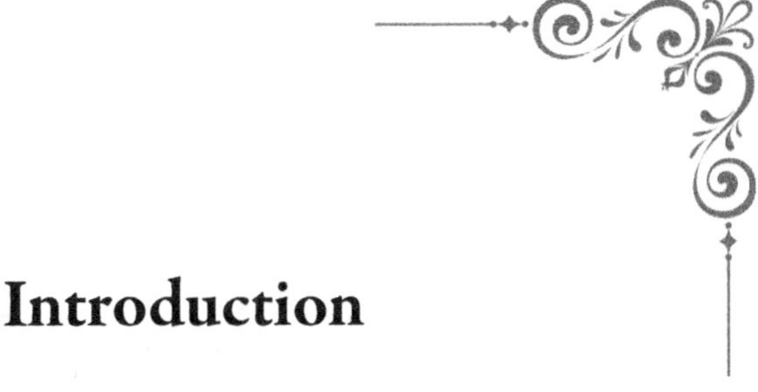

Introduction

In the shadows of our global society, a sinister network thrives, preying on the most vulnerable among us—our children. *Hidden Chains* delves into the harrowing realities of human trafficking, organ harvesting, illegal adoptions, and the fabrication of false identities and passport documents. This book exposes the dark underbelly of a system that repeatedly fails to protect those it is meant to safeguard.

Through meticulous research and heart-wrenching testimonies, *Hidden Chains* reveals how traffickers exploit legal loopholes and systemic weaknesses to perpetuate their heinous crimes. Children, stripped of their identities and rights, are reduced to mere commodities in a ruthless market driven by greed and desperation.

This book is not just a chronicle of suffering but a call to action. It seeks to illuminate the hidden chains that bind countless children worldwide, urging readers to confront the uncomfortable truths and advocate for systemic change. By understanding the complexities and failures of the current system, we can begin to forge a path towards justice and protection for the most innocent among us.

Chapter 1: Human Trafficking

Around the world there is numerous reports of missing persons on a daily basis. But do we know what happens to this missing persons or if they are ever found?

The most recent case that shook South Africa was the disappearance of little Joslin Smith who went missing. But how many more is there that we never hear of? And how can we as normal citizens stop this from happening?

Looking at the statistics is quite scary and some might think it's not that bad. Just because we don't hear or see it happening does not mean it doesn't exist.

https://www.state.gov/reports/2023-trafficking-in-persons-report/south-africa

SOUTH AFRICA (Tier 2 Watch List)

The Government of South Africa does not fully meet the minimum standards for the elimination of trafficking but is making significant efforts to do so. These efforts included increasing investigations and convictions of traffickers; investigating and prosecuting some allegedly complicit government officials; coordinating with foreign governments on trafficking investigations and repatriation of victims; increasing coordinated labour inspections to investigate forced labour; adopting an anti-trafficking NAP; accrediting two shelters; and expanding awareness-raising activities. However, the government did not demonstrate overall increasing efforts compared with the previous reporting period, even considering the impact of the COVID-19 pandemic, if any, on its anti-trafficking capacity. While the government finalized and approved the implementation regulations to operationalize the Prevention and Combating of Trafficking in Persons (PACOTIP) Act's immigration provisions, the regulations awaited final adoption and were not yet in effect at the end of the reporting period. Agencies responsible for identifying, referring, and certifying trafficking victims lacked coordination, and knowledge gaps in understanding human trafficking and referral SOPs, likely hindered overall protection efforts. Law enforcement continued to lack the necessary capacity and training to effectively identify and refer trafficking victims to care. The government inappropriately penalized victims solely for offenses committed as a direct result of being trafficked, including by detaining potential trafficking victims, even after identification as such by government officials, instead of referring them to care. Reports of low-level official complicity in trafficking crimes persisted. Because the government has devoted sufficient resources to a written plan that, if implemented, would constitute significant efforts to meet the minimum standards, South Africa was granted a waiver per the Trafficking Victims Protection Act from an otherwise required downgrade to Tier 3. Therefore South Africa remained on Tier 2 Watch List for the third consecutive year.

PRIORITIZED RECOMMENDATIONS:

Ensure victims are not inappropriately penalized solely for unlawful acts committed as a direct result of being trafficked.

Increase efforts to investigate, prosecute, and convict officials complicit in trafficking crimes and traffickers within organized crime syndicates, including cases of online exploitation.

Promulgate and implement the Department of Home Affairs (DHA) immigration provisions in chapters 3 and 7 of PACOTIP, including sections 15, 16, and 31(2)(b)(ii) to ensure the issuance of appropriate immigration status and identification documents for trafficking victims.

Increase training for South African Police Service (SAPS) officers on trauma-informed interviewing techniques as well as victim identification and referral SOPs, and train specialized investigators on human trafficking investigations and computer forensics to investigate online exploitation.

Increase resources and training for front-line responders to effectively use victim identification and referral SOPs to identify trafficking victims, including by screening for trafficking indicators among vulnerable populations, such as individuals engaging in commercial sex, children, LGBTQI+ persons, refugees, migrants, and Cuban medical workers, and systematically refer trafficking victims to care.

Increase collaboration between NICTIP, Provincial Task Teams (PTTs), and civil society to integrate referral and response systems and include all stakeholders, including survivors.

Implement policies to remove the requirement for victims to participate in investigations and prosecutions in order to be formally identified and receive trafficking victim status.

Formalize a confidential reporting mechanism for civil society to safely report allegations of official corruption and complicity in trafficking crimes directly to the government for vigorous investigation.

Accredit or establish additional shelters to accommodate the needs of male, LGBTQI+, and child trafficking victims.

Implement and consistently enforce strong regulations and oversight of labor recruitment companies, including by holding fraudulent labor recruiters criminally accountable.

Increase outreach and awareness efforts to vulnerable populations, especially for those engaging in commercial sex, in rural and agricultural communities, and foreign migrants.

PROSECUTION

The government maintained anti-trafficking law enforcement efforts. PACOTIP criminalized sex trafficking and labor trafficking and prescribed penalties of up to life imprisonment, a fine of up to 100 million South African rand ($5.9 million), or both. The penalties were sufficiently stringent and, with respect to sex trafficking, commensurate with those for other serious crimes, such as rape. The implementing regulations for PACOTIP's immigration provisions found in sections 15, 16, and 31(2)(b)(ii) were finalized and approved by the Minister of Home Affairs, but not yet formally adopted by parliament and promulgated; therefore, critical sections of the act remained inactive for the tenth consecutive year. The Criminal Law (Sexual Offenses and related matters) Amendment Act of 2007 (CLAA) also criminalized the sex trafficking of children and adults and prescribed penalties of up to life in prison. The Basic Conditions of Employment Act of 1997 (BCEA), amended in 2014, criminalized forced labour and prescribed maximum penalties of three to six years' imprisonment. In addition, the Children's Amendment Act of 2005 prescribed penalties of five years to life imprisonment or fines for the use, procurement, or offer of a child for slavery, commercial sexual exploitation, or to commit crimes. Prosecutors sometimes relied on the Prevention of Organized Crime Act of 1998, in combination with CLAA, which added additional charges – such as money laundering, racketeering, or criminal gang activity – and increased penalties of convicted defendants.

The Directorate for Priority Crime Investigation (DPCI, or Hawks), a division of SAPS, initiated 29 trafficking case investigations – 19 for sex trafficking, eight for labour trafficking, and two for unspecified forms of trafficking – and continued 35 case investigations from previous reporting periods. This compared with initiating 18 case investigations in the previous reporting period. The National Prosecuting Authority (NPA) initiated 15 prosecutions of 30 suspects and continued 28 prosecutions of 74 suspects from prior reporting periods, compared with nine prosecutions with 16 suspects during the previous reporting period. The government convicted 14 traffickers in eight cases, including two forced labour cases, under trafficking or immigration-related charges, compared with convicting 11 traffickers in the previous reporting period. Judges sentenced traffickers from 15 years to life imprisonment. The government reported two convictions were upheld on appeal and seven individuals were acquitted, which were appealed by the government and remained ongoing. The government initiated prosecutions of two South African traffickers for forced labour in agriculture; their associates, two Mozambican recruiters, fraudulently recruited and transported 39 victims, including children, from Mozambique and were convicted for illegal entry, which included a sentence of three months' imprisonment and a fine. The case remained ongoing.

The government recognized official complicity as a key challenge in addressing all transnational crime, including human trafficking, and investigated and prosecuted government officials during the reporting period. The government prosecuted the co-defendant of an acting judge, who was deceased before criminal proceedings began, for multiple trafficking-related crimes. The government charged three SAPS officers for extorting potential trafficking victims in a case reported in 2021; the case remained ongoing. Two NPA prosecutors were implicated in a potential corruption scheme for obstructing efforts to hold a high-profile, public figure accountable for alleged child sex trafficking over several years; the government did not report any actions taken against the prosecutors. Observers and government officials continued to report widespread corruption particularly among DHA, the Department of Social Development (DSD), SAPS, and DPCI. Observers reported high-level law enforcement officials obstructed trafficking investigations. DHA arrested 22 immigration officials for corruption related to facilitating illegal entry, transportation, and harbouring of foreign nationals. Observers also reported in exchange for bribes, lower-level officials warned traffickers of operations by law enforcement, immigration officials facilitated undocumented entry for traffickers at land and air border points, and DSD returned survivors to traffickers instead of referring them to care. Observers reported some SAPS officers were unwilling to investigate cases, particularly of children forced to engage in street vending or begging, and relied on NGOs to obtain victims' statements and build cases. Observers reported cases of sex trafficking of Basotho women from Lesotho in South African brothels; however, due to alleged official complicity of both Basotho and South African officials linked to the brothels, they continued to operate with impunity. Given mistrust in law enforcement, civil society reported the need for a trusted, high-level government contact to receive reports of officials complicit in human trafficking crimes to facilitate investigations and to avoid retribution. The government reported the existence of several secure mechanisms to report corruption, but did not specify if any were sensitive to the specific considerations of human trafficking crimes.

Law enforcement agencies lacked sufficient resources and training to adequately and appropriately investigate all reported trafficking cases. SAPS officers sometimes conflated GBV and human trafficking crimes. Observers reported law enforcement had insufficient training in trauma-informed interviewing and victim care, resulting in cases of DPCI investigators re traumatizing victims or not taking victims' statements. The lack of clarity on case status, low prospect of success, and sometimes years-long delays in cases dissuaded some victims from participating in trials. DPCI had a national anti-trafficking coordinator, four investigators to provide operational support, and provincial anti-trafficking coordinators in all nine districts; however, there were no officers or staff solely dedicated to anti-trafficking efforts. SAPS created an anti-trafficking unit within its General Detectives section, which primarily handled trafficking crimes involving adult victims. The SAPS family, child, and sexual offense unit handled trafficking crimes involving children. Observers reported SAPS did not collaborate with civil society and were reportedly slow to investigate leads generated by other law enforcement agencies. Media reports accused NPA of not proceeding with victims' cases in prior years because of discrimination due to disabilities or race.

With support from an international organization, the government trained more than 450 frontline law enforcement officers in Gauteng, Western Cape, and Eastern Cape provinces. An international organization supported DPCI to conduct a train-the-trainer training for 16 DPCI and SAPS officers to educate other officers on the SAPS trafficking SOPs. An international organization also supported NPA to train 100 prosecutors from eight provinces in three trainings. The government signed memoranda of understanding with the Governments of Mozambique, Botswana, Zambia, and Thailand for intelligence sharing and coordinating victim repatriations. The government coordinated with the Government of the Democratic Republic of the Congo (DRC) to investigate potential trafficking of

DRC migrants residing in the country. SAPS coordinated with the Lesotho Mounted Police Service on three cross-border investigations; however, SAPS officers sometimes did not effectively communicate with their counterparts.

PROTECTION

The government made uneven protection efforts. The government identified and referred 74 trafficking victims to care, including 42 labour trafficking victims, 23 sex trafficking victims, and nine victims of unspecified forms of trafficking, compared with identifying 83 victims and referring 74 victims to care in the previous reporting period. Of the 74 trafficking victims identified, 43 were foreign victims. NGOs identified and referred to care an additional 52 trafficking victims and identified 383 potential victims through transit monitoring. Observers reported official statistics did not reflect the scope of trafficking, since institutional problems and lack of proactive screening resulted in some victims remaining unidentified by the government. Conflation between GBV and human trafficking also led to the misidentification of victims.

In partnership with international organizations, the government trained social workers on victim identification, reporting, and referrals, particularly focused on combating online abuse and exploitation. Most agencies, including SAPS, DSD, NPA, and the Department of Justice and Constitutional Development (DOJCD), used SOPs adapted for each agency to identify and refer trafficking victims to care, developed in accordance with PACOTIP and support from an international organization; however, agencies and provinces implemented the SOPs inconsistently. Authorities inappropriately penalized victims of trafficking for offenses committed as a direct result of being trafficked, including for immigration offenses. As reported by multiple sources, trafficking victims were detained and deported after identification as trafficking victims and the government did not screen detained migrants for trafficking. During the reporting period, the government deported more than 800 Basotho, which included some trafficking victims. The government reportedly arrested and charged 52 undocumented migrants working in a single factory, including Malawians, Zimbabweans, and People's Republic of China (PRC) nationals, including some potential trafficking victims, for immigration violations; allegedly, these potential victims were charged and faced deportation after declining to participate with investigations, despite expressing fears of retaliation. The government arrested and charged 19 Bangladeshi potential trafficking victims with immigration violations after officials could not provide interpretation services and the potential victims declined to cooperate with investigations.

The government reported providing trafficking victims with temporary emergency shelter, food assistance, interpreters, specialized medical care, psycho-social support, and transportation. Observers reported the lack of training, awareness of agency responsibilities, and coordination by government officials resulted in victims facing delays in receiving care and increased the potential for victims returning to or being located by their traffickers. By law, trafficking victims were not required to participate in the investigation and prosecution of traffickers; however, in practice, to access services, many victims had to report to law enforcement. For certification as a trafficking victim – the process that permitted victims to access government services and benefits – victims must report their case to SAPS; SAPS was then required to confirm the trafficking allegations, file human trafficking charges within 48 hours, and coordinate with the provincial DSD representative. DSD was responsible for certifying trafficking victim status by issuing a letter of recognition, authorizing and monitoring the provision of protective services, preparing victim-witnesses for court, and accompanying victims through trial and repatriation, if applicable. Observers reported DSD and SAPS lacked coordination and were often unreachable to certify victims' status, resulting in victims sometimes unable to access timely emergency shelter and services, hindering overall protection efforts. DSD and SAPS disputed this characterization, claiming officials were available 24 hours a day, seven days a week. Observers reported instances of SAPS officers leaving trafficking victims at shelters without coordinating with DSD and, when this occurred in Gauteng and Western Cape, DSD refused assistance to victims until confirmation from SAPS was obtained. As reported by observers, in numerous instances, SAPS, DPCI, and DSD left victims at police stations overnight if their case was opened at the end of or after business hours. After reporting to SAPS, within the same 48-hour time period, victims had to decide whether to participate in criminal justice proceedings. Reportedly, victims willing to participate in investigations and prosecutions received certification and services faster than those unwilling to cooperate. To circumvent the existing process in Western Cape, DSD and the Department of Health (DOH) had SOPs that permitted medical and psychological assessments for victims before certification to access immediate care.

The government continued oversight of 18 NGO-run multipurpose shelters, operated one government multipurpose shelter that could assist trafficking victims, and accredited two new shelters; however, the accreditation of nine shelters to serve trafficking victims expired during the reporting period. These shelters continued providing services to trafficking victims. Each province had at least one accredited multipurpose shelter. Standards of care determined the accreditation status of shelters and accreditation lasted either two or four years before re-evaluation. Victims were not permitted to leave shelters without police escort but could discontinue shelter services at any time. Few shelters accepted victims with their children. Additionally, the government oversaw 88 NGO and government-operated semi-accredited shelters in compliance with DSD's minimum standards of care for trafficking victims that could provide emergency care for up to 72 hours. The government also operated a network of 61 Thuthuzela Care Centres (TCCs) –

full-service crisis centres to assist victims of GBV, including trafficking victims – adding six new TCCs during the reporting period. The government could provide shelter for unaccompanied child trafficking victims in Child and Youth Care Centres. Additional NGO-operated shelters, unaccredited by the government, also provided care specifically to trafficking victims. The government provided NGO-operated multi-purpose shelters a stipend on a per-person, per-night basis; however, these shelters reported funds were generally inaccessible after business hours, due to unresponsiveness by SAPS and DSD. Due to decreases in both government and private funding for NGO-operated shelters, numerous chronically underfunded shelters serving trafficking victims faced closure. The government maintained accreditation for one shelter serving male trafficking victims in Gauteng. Vulnerable populations, such as LGBTQI+ persons, particularly transgender persons and LGBTQI+ migrants, were especially at high risk for trafficking due to social stigmatization. Reportedly, two one-stop centres could provide shelter to LGBTQI+ victims, but available space was limited. Shelters accessible to persons with disabilities provided limited services; it was unknown if trafficking victims received these services during the reporting period. In Gauteng, trafficking victims could receive substance abuse treatment through five accredited treatment centers; treatment was provided for 12 weeks. The shelters in Gauteng, KwaZulu-Natal (KZN), and Western Cape generally offered adequate standards of care in both rural and urban areas, but quality of care in other provinces varied. Observers reported government shelter staff sometimes neglected to inform victims of the status of criminal cases against traffickers. Foreign victims, including both undocumented and with legal authorization, were fearful of accessing services at government facilities. Undocumented victims could not legally seek employment, even when cooperating with law enforcement, and their trials extended several years.

Through the NPA's Court Preparation Program, the government could provide victims with the option to testify via video conference both while in the country and after repatriation for foreign victims; and enhanced shelter and witness protection if the victim faced danger due to participation in the case. The government could provide interpretation for victims' oral testimony and translation for written statements. The government reported that all identified victims participated in criminal justice proceedings. NGOs emphasized the critical need for SAPS to issue Police Inquiry Numbers and CAS numbers to victims to facilitate follow-up on victim referrals and enable victims to track their cases. PACOTIP allowed judges to order victim restitution in trafficking cases, but the government did not report any orders during the reporting period.

Foreign victims faced additional barriers to access care and justice. PACOTIP authorized trafficking victims to receive relief from deportation. During the reporting period, the government finalized and approved regulations guiding the implementation of this provision and handling of trafficking cases; however, the regulations awaited final adoption by Parliament and were not yet in effect. As proscribed under PACOTIP, foreign trafficking victims were entitled to a visitor's visa for 30 days, which could be extended if cooperating in an investigation or prosecution or if danger to the victim exists in their home country; however, the government did not report issuing these visas. DHA had a policy to issue temporary identification documentation for foreign trafficking victims, requiring renewal every two weeks and continued cooperation with SAPS; however, DHA did not report providing such documentation to any trafficking victims. The Mpumalanga PTT coordinated with the Governments of Mozambique and Eswatini to repatriate trafficking victims, sometimes in partnership with an international organization.

PREVENTION

The government maintained mixed efforts to prevent trafficking. The government coordinated anti-trafficking efforts through NICTIP, which was chaired by DOJCD, with representatives from DHA, DSD, SAPS, NPA, DOH, Department of Employment and Labour (DOEL), Department of International Relations and Cooperation; with support from an international organization, NICTIP met regularly. NICTIP, with support from an international organization, drafted and approved its 2023-2026 National Policy Framework (NPF), soliciting input from select NGOs and one survivor, and allocated resources for its implementation. The government did not have a dedicated budget for anti-trafficking efforts, but individual agencies contributed to their respective anti-trafficking efforts. DOJCD allocated 1.7 million South African rand ($100,310) to support training efforts, implementation of the NPF, and NICTIP and some PTT meetings for 2023. The chair of NICTIP directed all governmental trafficking efforts and implementation of the NPF. DOJCD also chaired the National Rapid Response Team, which coordinated trafficking investigations and victim identifications and referrals; its activities were not reported. Established in all nine provinces, PTTs coordinated provincial policies and Provincial Rapid Response Teams (PRRTs) facilitated local responses to trafficking cases and victim identifications. As reported in previous years, some PTTs met regularly, including in KZN, Western Cape, Free State, and Mpumalanga, while others met sporadically. Representatives on both NICTIP and PTTs shared duties on multiple task teams for other crimes, such as GBV, which limited capacity and resources to address human trafficking. Observers previously reported SAPS, DHA, and DOEL were often absent from PTT and PRRT meetings, likely hindering overall efforts.

The government did not comprehensively monitor or investigate forced labour of adults or children in the agricultural, mining, construction, and fishing sectors and labor inspectors lacked necessary training to effectively identify trafficking. DOEL trained 48 inspectors on employment laws, human trafficking, and child exploitation in KZN. SAPS, DOEL, and DHA conducted joint inspections targeting child and forced labour; the joint task force referred several cases for investigation involving child labor and foreign trafficking victims, some of whom were penalized for immigration violations. While inspectors had the legal authority to investigate private farms, they reported difficulty in securing access. For the past three years, observers reported DHA did not often provide vulnerable migrant populations with proper immigration documentation, resulting in children denied entry to schools, which increased vulnerabilities for trafficking. The government did not effectively regulate foreign labour recruiters or penalize them for fraudulent recruitment. Although the law prohibited worker-paid recruitment fees, the government's limited capacity hindered its ability to enforce this provision, especially in the informal sector. SAPS operated a crime hotline that could receive reports of potential trafficking cases and a mobile app that led to 19 investigations with one confirmed trafficking case. The government and civil society directed most trafficking-related calls to the NGO-operated National Human Trafficking Hotline (NHTH), which the government advertised. In cooperation with PRRTs, NHTH received 3,374 calls pertaining to human trafficking in 2022, identified 391 potential victims, and successfully assisted with the removal of 50 trafficking victims from exploitation. Observers reported most calls to the NHTH from victims occurred after police neglected to take their reports seriously or alleged police complicity was involved. An NGO-operated national social justice hotline also received calls concerning human trafficking.

The government conducted awareness-raising activities in KZN, Free State, Gauteng, Eastern Cape, North West, Northern Cape, and Western Cape provinces, in collaboration with international organizations, reaching more than 84,000 individuals. DSD partnered with a taxi union to raise awareness of trafficking among taxi drivers and commuters. DPCI focused on raising awareness in vulnerable communities. PTTs in four provinces conducted anti-trafficking awareness activities. The government's efforts to implement a previously reported integrated data collection system faced challenges and the government remained without means to collect human trafficking-related data. The South African National Defense Forces maintained a hotline for reports of sexual exploitation by armed forces but did not report whether it received any calls regarding such exploitation during the reporting period. Since 2015, 58 allegations of sexual exploitation and 10 allegations of sexual abuse were made against 67 South African peacekeepers; of these, the government has taken accountability measures in 22 cases and continued investigating six other cases. The Generic and Sector Specific Training Manual on the PACOTIP Act contained a training plan for peacekeepers; however, the government did not report providing anti-trafficking training to its troops prior to deployment as peacekeepers. The government did not make efforts to reduce the demand for commercial sex acts. The government reported training its diplomatic personnel on transnational crimes, but not specifically on identifying trafficking indicators.

TRAFFICKING PROFILE:

As reported over the past five years, human traffickers exploit domestic and foreign victims in South Africa, and traffickers exploit victims from South Africa abroad. Traffickers recruit victims from neighbouring countries and rural areas within South Africa, particularly Gauteng, and exploit them in sex trafficking locally and in urban centres, such as Johannesburg, Cape Town, Durban, and Bloemfontein. Traffickers force both adults and children, particularly those from socioeconomically disadvantaged communities and rural areas as well as migrants, into labour in domestic service, mining, food services, construction, criminal activities, agriculture, and the fishing sector. Traffickers may exploit South Africans in forced labour on vineyards and fruit and vegetable farms across the country.

High unemployment and socioeconomic stratification increased vulnerability of exploitation, particularly of youth, Black women, and foreign migrants. Traffickers recruit victims who are unemployed and struggle with substance use, and commonly use substances to maintain control of victims, including children. Parents with drug addictions sometimes exploit their children in sex trafficking to pay for drugs. Traffickers increasingly entice foreign and South African women and girls with the promise of marriage and then force them into labour after marriage. Abuse of the custom of ukuthwala, a cultural norm that can manifest into forced marriage, may contribute to vulnerability of girls and women to exploitation, particularly in Eastern Cape and KZN. According to a study, in 2021, approximately 500,000 children dropped out of school, resulting in a total of 750,000 children not enrolled in school; high death rates from the pandemic increased the orphan population, leaving more children vulnerable to exploitation. There were some reports of boys lured out of the country for fake sports scholarships and then forced into exploitation.

Traffickers recruit both foreign and South African victims through fake job advertisements on social media and classified advertisement forums, including advertisements for webcam modelling, hospitality, mining, and domestic work. Some fake advertisements, particularly for domestic work, specifically request Zimbabwean or Malawian applicants. Some farmers rely on "bakkie brokers" to rapidly expand their personnel during harvest season, bringing foreign migrants to work on farms; these brokers are unregulated and charge workers recruitment fees. Traffickers exploit young men from neighbouring countries who migrate to South Africa for farm work; some are subsequently arrested and deported as undocumented immigrants. Despite high unemployment, migrants travel from East, Central, and Southern Africa to South Africa looking for economic opportunity, particularly from Ethiopia and Mozambique, and are vulnerable to exploitation. The lack of valid documentation, due to a protracted asylum process, limited asylum seeker's ability to access protection and services.

Official complicity in trafficking crimes, especially by police and immigration officials, facilitated the operation of traffickers and organized syndicates engaging in trafficking. Syndicates, predominantly operated by Nigerians, force women from Nigeria and countries bordering South Africa into commercial sex, primarily in brothels and other commercial-front establishments. South African organized trafficking syndicates exploit girls as young as 10 years old in sex trafficking. Some well-known brothels, previously identified as locations of sex trafficking, continue to operate with officials' tacit approval. In some cases, traffickers exploit women in brothels disguised as guesthouses. Syndicates also recruit South African women to Europe, where traffickers force some into sex trafficking, domestic service, or drug smuggling. Mozambican crime syndicates use the eastern border of Kruger National Park in Mpumalanga, enabled by corrupt officials, to transport migrants to other parts of the country for forced labour, through the same routes used by syndicates to facilitate other crimes. Syndicates also exploit miners, both South African and foreign migrants, sometimes known as zama zamas, in illegal gold, diamond, and coal mining; miners are exposed to dangerous conditions and sometimes killed by gangs vying for control of mines. Traffickers operating in South Africa are mostly from Nigeria and South Africa; however, there were reports of traffickers from Bangladesh, Tanzania, Malawi, Mozambique, Pakistan, Zimbabwe, Ethiopia, and the PRC.

Undocumented children, including child trafficking victims from Mozambique, the DRC, and Zimbabwe, are unable to access education and government services, which increases their risk of statelessness and vulnerability to trafficking. Recruiters entice women from the Middle

East, Asia, and countries bordering South Africa with offers of legitimate employment but, upon arrival, some subject the women to domestic servitude or forced labor in the service sector. Traffickers exploit Basotho women in sex trafficking and domestic servitude and men in labor trafficking, particularly in the mining and textile sectors, in South Africa. Traffickers exploit foreign male victims aboard fishing vessels in South Africa's territorial waters. Asian workers may travel to South Africa via commercial flights to disembark on fishing vessels where they are exploited. Traffickers subject Pakistanis and Bangladeshis to forced labour through debt-based coercion in businesses owned by their co-nationals. Owners of privately-owned PRC businesses exploit PRC nationals, South African, and Malawian adults and children in factories, sweatshops, and other businesses. There were 432 Cuban medical workers in South Africa at the end of 2022. Authorities continued to partner with the Government of Cuba to hire medical professionals to provide services in all provinces. South African officials indicated workers were in control of their passports and credentials and reported contracting and paying workers directly. However, it was unclear if Cuban workers controlled their own bank accounts and there was no information on the contracts the workers signed with the Cuban government. In 2022, a credible international NGO published a global report on the Cuban labour export program, in which 18 former workers provided testimony on the conditions faced in South Africa. According to the report, 45 percent were under surveillance, 48 percent were subjected to movement restrictions, 80 percent reported exploitation, 72 percent reported threats and violence, and 50 percent reported being forced to enroll in the program by Cuban authorities.

This is a actual report of 2023 but still this is what is reported and known. How many people is trafficked without anyone ever knowing?

In South Africa, the extent of sexual exploitation of children has increased drastically and its nature has changed over time. On a regular basis, there are reports of cases of children rescued from human traffickers and from the clutches of sex slave rings.

While some of the stories are reported by the media, there are several other cases that go unreported due to the secretive and criminal nature of the activities. A common feature in the cases is that young children, mostly girls, are used as sex slaves and for other commercial purposes by trafficking rings. Even more shocking is the fact that several of the victims are children between the ages of 10 and 14 years old. The cases of sexual exploitation of children in South Africa reflect a new dimension and a growing trend in the pattern of child exploitation in the country. The more concerning aspect is the desensitisation of the society to the sexual exploitation of, and trafficking of children.

SOCIAL IMPACTS AND THE MANIFESTATIONS OF SEC

Sexual Exploitation of Children (SEC) creates a culture that considers children as possessions to be used, with no consideration for their well-being. As the victims are exploited through numerous means, SEC manifests in various forms. The most common manifestations and most closely linked forms of SEC in South Africa are exploitation through prostitution, pornography, child sex trafficking, online sexual exploitation of children and sex for a favour by adults.

Using psychological manipulation, the perpetrators of SEC lure victims into sex slavery through promises of a better education/ jobs, family protection and economic support. The perpetrators also recruit victims by promising their families they will be better taken care of by means of cash paid to the family through the child's earnings.

A growing form of sexual exploitation of children In South Africa is "survival sex". This is a situation where sex is exchanged for basic necessities such as food, shelter, education or to settle a debt owed by a family member.

Furthermore, the increasing cross-border movement of people and new technologies have enabled the sexual exploitation of children to evolve and manifest in new forms.

The internet has made it easier and less expensive to possess and disseminate images of sexual contents with children involved, both locally and across international borders. With high returns and low risk, this makes online child sexual exploitation as well as child trafficking a lucrative business. The increasing number of children crossing the borders to South Africa unaccompanied has increased the number of children vulnerable to exploitation and trafficking. Mozambique and Zimbabwe, followed by Malawi, Swaziland and Lesotho are the major countries of origin for unaccompanied children and children on the move.

On 24 January, EUROSTAT published the 2022 statistics for trafficking in human beings. The newly released data show that 10,093 victims of trafficking in human beings were registered in the EU in 2022, representing a 41% increase compared to 2021. This increase may be the result of higher detection rates of victims thanks, among other things, to awareness raising actions across the EU in 2022 to prevent trafficking of those fleeing the military aggression against Ukraine.

Similarly to 2021, more than half of all the victims in the EU are women and girls (63%). In the cases where the victim's age group is known, children make up 15% of the victims. This represents a drop compared to 2021. The majority of child victims are female (75%).

The share of EU nationals among the registered victims is 37%, representing a significant decrease compared to 2021. Across the EU, approximately 25% of all registered victims are citizens of the country in which they were registered, which constitutes a 19% decrease compared to 2021.

For the first time, the number of registered victims for labour exploitation (3,990) came close to the number of victims sexually exploited (4,014), each amounting to about 41%. Trafficking for other purposes – criminal activities, forced begging, organ removal and others – reached a total of 1,699 victims (18% of all trafficking victims).

The number of suspected traffickers decreased by 16% (8,064 in total) and the number of convicted traffickers decreased by almost 17% (2,097) in 2022 compared to 2021.

Chapter 2 Cases in the news

Friday, February 2, 2024

A multi-disciplinary team consisting of various units within the South African Police Service (SAPS), led by the Anti-Kidnapping Task Team, has arrested six suspects on suspicion of human trafficking and kidnapping in Mayfair, Johannesburg.

The six men are expected to face charges of human trafficking, sex trafficking, kidnapping and extortion. They are expected to appear before court today.

Two Indian women, aged between 20 and 24 years, have since been rescued.

The team, consisting of private security, received intelligence on a Johannesburg-based human trafficking network preying on Indian women.

The women were allegedly enticed to the country with false promises of employment. Upon arrival, they were kept against their will, offered to clients leading to sexual encounters.

On Wednesday, members operationalised information and pounced on an identified address and a commercial site.

The members seized an array of cell phones, numerous documents, including passports and cash, for further investigation. Investigations are continuing. – SAnews.gov.za

Human trafficking in SA: Hawks raise alarm in Gauteng

Provincial head of the Hawks in Gauteng, Major-General Ebrahim Kadwa, has raised an alarm over the rising cases of human trafficking in the province.

Kadwa said this is due to the province being an economic hub, among other factors.

He said the Hawks had intensified its response to information relating to human trafficking and smuggling of immigrants in the last three years, and has managed to crack some big cases.

The Hawks have also been raiding private premises and finding a number of trafficked people.

"In the recent cases, we found over 100 people initially reported, victims of trafficking. But there is a process we have to follow to be able to differentiate if it is human trafficking or we're dealing with organised illegal immigration or smuggling of migrants. This is a meticulous procedure that needs to be followed by the Hawks," he told Newsroom Afrika.

Human trafficking cases

Some of the big cases include the more than 15 undocumented immigrants who were found up at a gated Centurion estate last week:

October 2023 – Mother and son Dumazile Nkosi, 51, and Thandoluhle Nkosi, 25, were arrested after 47 foreign nationals were found in the premises they were leasing in Gauteng

November 2023 – A 28-year-old suspect for human trafficking was arrested after 23 Somalians were found in minibus taxis in Limpopo

December 2023 – A woman was arrested after three young girls had been trafficked from West Africa into South Africa inside a shipping container. They were advertised on an escort website and kept in a residential complex in George

December 2023 – 33 suspected human trafficking victims were rescued after they were found stashed in one room at a house in Benoni

December 2023 – Two suspects, a man, 46, and woman, 41, were seen boarding a bus in Midrand with 14 undocumented kids aged between 6 and 14 years

December 2023 – More than 130 undocumented men, women, and children travelling in 11 vehicles were intercepted by the Limpopo Provincial Tracking Team outside Polokwane

December 2023 – The Border Management Authority (BMA) said it intercepted 443 unaccompanied Zimbabwean children below the age of 8 years.

'Lucrative business'

According to Kadwa, human trafficking and the smuggling of people constitute a global criminal enterprise that is lucrative both internationally and in South Africa.

"We're not dealing with a single group. We are dealing with different groups from different regions that are operating in South Africa and targeting areas like Gauteng for issues such as sex trafficking, labour trafficking and other forms of trafficking that we are dealing with," he said.

He said that trafficking kingpins also Invest money into their operations, targeting the poor and those in unstable countries.

"Organised illegal migration networks are global. The masterminds are able to exploit people from poor backgrounds to go to these communities and recruit a whole army of these people, take them to Home Affairs so they can substitute these people through a whole scheme with the idea that they're going to be sent overseas."

"This is a vast network. We're dealing with kingpins and major players in this area with global connections." While the Hawks have managed to crack some of these cases, having arrested kingpins and middle-men, Kadwa admitted more still needed to be done to curb human trafficking in the country.

Hawks head Lt-Gen Godfrey Lebeya says South Africa has not been spared from the twin pandemics of human trafficking and smuggling of migrants.

"Trafficking in persons is described as modern-day slavery and a crime against humanity," he said.

He said during the reporting period for the third quarter of 2023/2024 , 19 potential victims of human trafficking were rescued.

Lebeya said three foreign nationals were convicted and four suspects were arrested.

Sixteen awareness campaigns were conducted and 17 disruptive operations conducted.

Lebeya outlined the progress made in the third quarter, taking stock of milestones achieved since the previous quarter.

He detailed a case where human trafficking suspects were arrested with 14 children on December 6 2023.

The Hawks multidisciplinary team, Kimberley family violence, child protection and sexual offences unit and Kimberley crime prevention arrested two Zimbabwean nationals on allegations of trafficking in persons.

In 2021, the Gauteng Department of Health came under the spotlight with Independent Media putting questions to it, over rumours of trafficking through some of its hospitals and the Department of Social Development, who also get a mention in the TIP report this year. We are still waiting for answers ...

The only mitigating factor preventing South Africa being downgraded to a Tier 3 country – the worst of the offenders – is because the country has a written plan that, "if implemented, would constitute significant efforts to meet the minimum standards".

The report details the efforts government has made in dealing with those that are identified, through either prosecuting the perpetrators or providing care for victims. The numbers shown, though, reflect only a margin of the scale of the problem itself.

Authors Notes

Personally I believe that this statistics is only an estimate. The "plans" that the Government has looks good on paper but as with many other problems the "plans" is never put into action.

In the meantime we as the people of a country can not keep turning a blind eye just because we think this won't happen to us. The statistics show 10 000 people go missing per month that's 120 000 per year.

1 in 3 trafficking cases is children. I'm not going to paint a pretty picture to what happens with this children when they are taken. It's time that the world sees what we allow because we keep quite and turn a blind eye. We try and protect ourselves from seeing the truth, but what about that poor children? Each child is someone's daughter, son, brother, sister. Every child has a heart, blood in its veins with feelings.

When this children gets taken they change hands approximately 15 times in an hour.

Chapter 3 Psychological effects

https://www.ncbi.nlm.nih.gov/ pmc/articles/ PMC5843209/

PMCID: PMC5843209PMID: 29518168

Psychological consequences of child trafficking: An historical cohort study of trafficked children in contact with secondary mental health services

Livia Ottisova, Conceptualization, Formal analysis, Investigation, Methodology, Project administration, Writing – original draft, Writing – review & editing,1,* Patrick Smith, Conceptualization, Supervision, Writing – review & editing,1 Hitesh Shetty, Investigation, Software,2 Daniel Stahl, Formal analysis, Methodology,3 Johnny Downs, Validation,4 and Sian Oram, Conceptualization, Methodology, Supervision, Writing – review & editing5

Michael L. Goodman, Editor

Author information Article notes Copyright and License information PMC Disclaimer

Background

Child trafficking is the recruitment and movement of people aged younger than 18 for the purposes of exploitation. Research on the mental health of trafficked children is limited, and little is known about the use of mental health services by this group. This study aimed to investigate the mental health and service use characteristics of trafficked children in contact with mental health services in England.

Methods & findings

The study employed an historical cohort design. Electronic health records of over 250,000 patients were searched to identify trafficked children, and a matched cohort of non-trafficked children was randomly selected. Data were extracted on the socio-demographic and clinical characteristics, abuse history, and trafficking experiences of the trafficked children. Logistic and linear random effects regression models were fitted to compare trafficked and non-trafficked children on their clinical profiles and service use characteristics. Fifty-one trafficked children were identified, 78% were female. The most commonly recorded diagnoses for trafficked children were post-traumatic stress disorder (PTSD) (22%) and affective disorders (22%). Records documented a high prevalence of physical violence (53%) and sexual violence (49%) among trafficked children. Trafficked children had significantly longer duration of contact with mental health services compared to non-trafficked controls (b = 1.66, 95% CI 1.09–2.55, p<0.02). No significant differences were found, however, with regards to pathways into care, prevalence of compulsory psychiatric admission, length of inpatient stays, or changes in global functioning.

Conclusions

Child trafficking is associated with high levels of physical and sexual abuse and longer duration of contact with mental health services. Research is needed on most effective interventions to promote recovery for this vulnerable group.

isk [8[1]–10[2]]. However, relatively little is known about the mental health needs of trafficked children, and even less is known about those with serious mental illnesses.

The only study to date conducted with a clinical population of trafficked people in contact with mental health services found that trafficked adults were significantly more likely to be compulsorily admitted as inpatients and had longer admissions than matched non-trafficked controls. However, whether or how the mental health needs of trafficked children in contact with services differ from those of non-trafficked children is currently not known.

This study aimed to investigate the sociodemographic and clinical characteristics of trafficked children in contact with secondary mental health services, and compare their pathways into services and current care with those of matched non-trafficked children. It was hypothesised that trafficked children, as compared to non-trafficked controls, would be (1) significantly more likely to have adverse pathways into care, defined as having first contact with secondary mental health services via the emergency department or police; (2) significantly more likely to be compulsorily admitted for psychiatric treatment (i.e. admitted for care under the Mental Health Act (MHA)); (3) have longer total length of contact with secondary mental health services and (4) longer inpatient admissions; and (5) would have significantly worse clinical outcomes as evidenced by less improvement in measures of global functioning.

---

1.   https://www.ncbi.nlm.nih.gov/pmc/articles/PMC5843209/#pone.0192321.ref008

2.   https://www.ncbi.nlm.nih.gov/pmc/articles/PMC5843209/#pone.0192321.ref010

And then we move on to how does trafficking happen in the first place? What is the stages to trafficking?

Trafficking of children is a form of human trafficking and is defined by the United Nations as the "recruitment, transportation, harbouring, and/or receipt" kidnapping of a child for the purpose of slavery, forced labour, and exploitation.[1]: Article 3© This definition is substantially wider than the same document's definition of "trafficking in persons".[1]: Article 3(a) Children may also be trafficked for adoption. Not all adoption is a form of human trafficking, but illegal or informal is. Illegal adoptions violate multiple child rights norms and principles, including the best interests of the child, the principle of subsidiarity and the prohibition of improper financial gain[2].

Though statistics regarding the magnitude of child trafficking are difficult to obtain, the International Labour Organization (ILO) estimates that 10,000 children are trafficked each year.[3] In 2012, the United Nations Office on Drugs and Crime (UNODC) reported the percentage of child victims had risen in 3 years from 20 percent to 27 percent.[4] Every year 300,000 children are taken from all around the world and sold by human traffickers as slaves. 28% of the 17,000 people brought to the United States are children—about 13 children per day.[5] In 2014, research conducted by the anti-human trafficking organization Thorn reported that internet sites like Craigslist are often used as tools for conducting business within the industry and that 70 percent of child sex trafficking survivors surveyed were at some point sold online.[6] The trafficking of children has been internationally recognized as a serious crime that exists in every region of the world and which often has human rights implications. Yet, it is only within the past decade that the prevalence and ramifications of this practice have risen to international prominence, due to a dramatic increase in research and public action. Limited research has not yet identified all causes of child trafficking, however, it appears that poverty, humanitarian crisis, and lack of education contribute to high rates. A variety of potential solutions have accordingly been suggested and implemented, which can be categorized into four types of action: broad protection, prevention, law enforcement, and victim assistance.[7][8]

10 Causes of Human Trafficking

The United Nations defines human trafficking[1] as "the recruitment, transportation, transfer, harbouring, or receipt of people through force, fraud, or deception, with the aim of exploiting them for profit." It exists in almost every industry, including domestic work, agriculture, mining, fishing, factory work, and commercial sex work. Victims of human trafficking can also be forced into marriage and armed conflict. Victims may be paid (they often aren't), but their wages are so low, they are essentially slaves. Why does human trafficking exist? Understanding the roots of trafficking can help the world address it. Here are ten of the primary causes:

#1. Poverty

#2. A lack of education

#3. The demand for cheap labour/sex

#4. A lack of human rights protections

#5. A lack of legitimate economic opportunities

#6. Cultural factors

#7. Conflict and natural disasters

#8. A lack of safe migration options

#9. Deception and intimidation

#10. Profit

Child trafficking differs from human trafficking in that no force or deception needs to take place in order to prove that a child has been

---

1. https://www.unodc.org/unodc/en/human-Trafficking/Human-Trafficking.html

trafficked. This difference is based on the fact that a child is considered incapable of taking an informed decision.

Chapter 4 Real stories of survivors

My Name Is Brooke Axtell and I Was Sex Trafficked at Age 7 in the US

I hated the fact that the abuse and trafficking I suffered growing up made me so vulnerable to more abuse and pain. I hated the fact that I trusted someone to help me when I was all alone in a new city. I hated the ways that I longed for safety and for someone to care. And most of all, at that moment, I hated the fact that I was still alive and that I had survived my childhood.

As a young child, I was sexually abused by family members, which then progressed to me being given to child pornographers. Shortly after the child pornography started, they began to sell my body to countless men and other pimps in suburban neighbourhoods. I was trafficked domestically in Canada, just as I was often taken to the USA and other international countries for the sole purpose of being trafficked.

I remember the smells, the sights, and the tastes of slavery. Silently the tears flow. The horror can't be put into words, neither can the brothels I was taken to or the men and women I was forced to service. Not only did I see someone very close to me murdered, but police officers were some of my buyers and multiple times I was handcuffed, raped, and told that if I told anyone I would be put in jail. I was scared to reach out for help and growing up the message that was branded on my heart was the idea that I had no worth, I was shameful, and all I was good for was sex.

IN HER OWN WORDS: WRITER and Survivor Advocate Brooke Axtell

"Real women. Real stories."

By Brooke Axtell

December 12, 2016

THIS STORY IS PART of the "Real Women, Real Stories," series called a social project designed to promote awareness of the often unseen hardships women face in different professions and places around the world. You can contribute to the project here.

Last year, at the 2015 Grammy Awards, I collaborated with pop singer Katy Perry and President Obama to address the issue of gender violence. After the President highlighted the White House "It's On Us" campaign, I was invited to speak.

I shared my personal story of overcoming domestic violence and how I found healing. I encouraged those struggling with the pain of abuse to reach out for help. But what I didn't share that night was how my history of early sexual assault and child sex trafficking prepared me to accept partner violence as an adult.

Like many survivors of domestic violence, my abuse started long before I met my then-boyfriend. Sexual exploitation trained me to believe I was unworthy of the love I so desperately craved.

I was 7 years old when I was trafficked for sex.

My favourite colour was pink and I loved to dance. My room was filled with books, dolls and art. I read for hours on my white chair surrounded by stuffed animals, listening to my white music box with the delicate roses and gold edges.

When I took baths, I would rest on my back and sing my first song, "Flying wings, angel sing, strawberry dreams." Over and over I would sing the same chorus, moving my arms like an angel. Hanging from the bathroom wall was a framed scripture from the book of I Samuel. It is known as Hannah's Prayer, but in this version, my name replaced the son she prays for. The calligraphy read, "I have prayed for this child, Brooke, and the Lord has granted me what I have asked of him, so now I give her to the Lord for her whole life she will be given over to him."

My mom taught me God is love. But she was in the hospital and I feared she would never return. My dad travelled for work to take care of our family, so I also had a nanny.

My nanny talked about God, too. He said it was God's will for him to punish me for my sins. What punishment did I deserve? He did not say the word and I did not have language for what was happening. I could not tell anyone what his deity demanded on my white iron bed with the pink sheets.

He called me a "worthless whore" and said I made him do this to me. When he raped me, repeating the Lord's prayer, I flew outside my body. Sometimes his voice still echoes within me, "Deliver us from evil. Deliver us from evil." A part of me split off to survive, to guard the truth, to carry the unbearable weight of this. I multiplied and disappeared.

The first rape was my Initiation, my rite of passage into his underworld. A place filled with secrets and shadows, people with dead eyes.

From that initial violation, he secretly took me to houses, hotels, and parties to sell me to men for sex. I was forced into pornography with adults and other children. I was caged and taunted like a trapped animal.

When they filmed me I flew outside my body to take refuge in the beautiful worlds I created: one with a white horse, one where I danced with the angels. Each time they invaded me, I soared above them. I was passed from man to man, hand to hand, like a doll. My soul travelled and retreated, crossed oceans, centuries. I lived a thousand lives in a single night.

This rhythm continued. During the day, I attended school. At night, I belonged to him — and whoever was interested in buying me.

The buyers were always wealthy white men who were insatiable in their appetite to inflict pain. I numbed myself, circling my life as if it belonged to someone else. I became a spectator of the abuse. This is happening to some other little girl, the evil one, who needed to be punished, I told myself. I created a wall, so I could live on the light side, be the good one and continue without pain.

Finally, my mom came home from the hospital in a wheelchair. I was too terrified and ashamed to reveal the abuse, but she sensed something was wrong. She listened to her intuition and fired my nanny.

The exploitation ended suddenly, but my shame did not. No matter how much I accomplished in life, I was still haunted by his lie about me, "Worthless, worthless, worthless."

I lived for many years concealing the secret of my trauma. What I witnessed felt unspeakable.

Faced with an abusive boyfriend as an adult, I sought out help from a brilliant counsellor specializing in sexual violence and resolving developmental trauma. It was there, with her, that I finally felt safe enough to admit what had happened to me — beyond the domestic abuse— and find my healing path.

Eventually, through therapy, an inspiring community of other survivors, and my own creative expression through poetry and music, I found my way back to my original worth. But my recovery has also given me a greater understanding of sex trafficking and how it's perpetuated.

We live in a culture where women and girls are reduced to sexual commodities, where sexual and domestic violence are not aberrations. For many of us, they are rites of passage, the training ground for internalizing our own oppression.

Child sex trafficking is part of this continuum of violence. It is rape for profit. The appearance of consent is merely a performance the child must enact to survive. Even if a child is actively trading sex for money, food or shelter to survive, this still qualifies as statutory rape. There is no such thing as a child sex worker or child prostitute. There is only child rape.

It Is easy to blame those who profit from the exploitation of children — as well we should. But they are not the whole problem. In a country where one out of six American women are survivors of sexual assault and one out of four women are survivors of domestic violence, traffickers are simply monetizing a culture that normalizes violence against women and girls at epidemic rates. This brutal reality along with the pervasive cult of victim-blaming has created the perfect marketplace for the buying and selling of children.

In my work as an advocate, I've learned that facing the truth is the beginning of freedom. To be free, we have to bring everything into the light, so our shame and our secrets no longer have power over us. As survivors, we may never see our perpetrators held accountable for their crimes, but we are creating our own justice. Our justice is to overcome, to know our worth, to rise up as leaders, transforming pain into the power of compassion.

Chapter 5 Adoptions

Adoptions is often a life saver to many children across the world, but it can also be the worst thing that ever happen to them. Let's explore Adoptions and how it is linked to trafficking and exploitation of our most vulnerable, our children.

Within our law system to sell a child is illegal and you can get jail sentenced.

2.4 What do people mean when they say that a child is being "trafficked"?

Trafficking in relation to a child means the recruitment, sale, supply, transportation, transfer, harbouring or receipt of children, within or across the borders of South Africa. This can be done by any means, including: the use of threats, force or other forms of coercion; abduction; fraud; deception; abuse of power; or the giving or receiving of payments or benefits to achieve the consent of a person having control of a child. It can also be done because of a position of vulnerability on the side of the child. All of this must be done for the purposes of exploiting the child, and it can also include the adoption of a child facilitated or secured through illegal means.

In essence when you sell a child it is called trafficking. But yet people pay social services to adopt children. The average cost to adopt a child can be anything between R60 000 - R100 000. Also in some instances the state pays NPO or NGO organisations to perform this adoptions.

This caused mass removal of children from hospitals and new born babies was taken from their mother's at birth. Children under the age of five would be removed from their parental homes with false allegations, hearsay evidence and falsified or illegal documents. Often parents are then forced into signing adoption papers by method of blackmail.

One of such cases was placed in a news paper article, but there is many more such cases.

Published May 25, 2024

A young mother's life has been torn apart after an official of a child adoption organisation allegedly forced her to give up her five-month-old son.

In what appears to be a growing illegal child adoption scandal in South Africa, Nomalanga* claims she was blackmailed into signing adoption papers of her baby.

IN A CONSENT FORM, rubber stamped by the Department of Social Development (DSD) dated April 16, it states that Nomalanga voluntarily consented to the adoption of her son, Tumelo*.

Tumelo is currently living at a children's home after he was allegedly taken away from her on suspicion of her doing drugs, an allegation Nomalanga denies.

The document reads in part: "I can hereby voluntarily consent to the adoption of the said child to a person or persons unknown to me."

However, speaking exclusively to The Saturday Star, 21-year-old Nomalanga claims she was blackmailed into signing the papers.

She said an official, known to The Saturday Star, from a Brakpan non-profit-organisation (NPO), Rata Social Services, told her if she did not give away the baby she was also going to lose her two-year-old first-born daughter.

This, after the official accused her of doing drugs and "sleeping around".

TELLING HER STORY TO The Star, Nomalanga, who lives with her parents in Brakpan, said her ordeal started a few days after she gave birth to Tumelo.

"After I gave birth I felt sick and my mother suggested I take the children away so I can take care of myself. So her grandmother took care of the eldest and Tumelo went to stay with one of my mother's best friends so she could take proper care of him.

"Unfortunately, when I went to fetch my child she told me someone else was taking care of him, to my surprise," Nomalanga said.

SHE SAID HER MOTHER'S best friend eventually told her she had given her son up for adoption without her consent. However after inquiries from Nomalanga, Tumelo was put in a children's home, known to The Star

Yesterday, Nomalanga was able to withdraw the adoption consent form she had signed.

"I truly feel that there is something else at play here. There is something happening, because the day I reported that my child could be missing, I received a call from the Rata official to suggest I give my child up for adoption.

"I DON'T DO DRUGS. I also don't drink. Yes I'm young but I'm a fit mother," she said.

Asked where the child's father was, Nomalanga said he had walked away before the child was born. She confirmed that the same man fathered both children.

The DSD did not respond to questions sent by The Saturday Star

SPEAKING TO THE STAR, one of the owners of the centre, also known to The Saturday Star, where Tumelo is kept, vouched for Nomalanga, saying she did not do drugs and the child was healthy and strong.

"The child is doing well. He is about to be six months old in June, which means he will start eating proper food," he said.

Investigations by The Saturday Star found that by law, consent of both parents is mandatory in giving up a child for adoption.

ACCORDING TO THAT LAW, adoption refers to a situation whereby a child's legal relationship with their birth parents has ended and the child has become a legal member of a new family. Forced adoption is the removal of a child without the consent of their parents.

Rata Social Services NPC is an NPO focusing on children at risk, rendering preventative and statutory services.

Their landline rang unanswered.

Further cases that was reported and in articles shows how this illegal adoptions happens.

Private prosecution unit ends cruel exploits of alleged adoption scammer

Document type: Web page copy

Source: www.sapeople.com

Publication date: 1 June 2023

What started as a complaint from the Leithgöb family about the slow progress on their criminal case against the accused, and following the PPU's involvement, culminated in the police identifying dozens more victims of the alleged scam.

Van den Berg is alleged to have offered services as an adoption social worker, where she would charge prospective adoptive parents, many incapable of having children, for various services in the process to adopt a child. It is alleged that the accused did this, when in fact there was no child to adopt or a child had been offered to the hopeful parents, despite the biological mother not giving consent for adoption. Her alleged offences date back to 2014.

When the PPU took on the case, the police were only investigating a charge of fraud. In a letter in May last year, Adv. Gerrie Nel, head of the PPU, advised the investigating officer on the serious nature of the alleged offences. "We are concerned that more babies have been sold under similar circumstances that the complainant had to endure.

The prevalence of such conduct does raise serious consideration that the suspect's alleged behaviour could be likened to and fall within the ambit of trafficking.

"Furthermore, the suspect seems to be continuing with her devious manipulation because of the vulnerability of childless people. Decisive investigation and action by the South African Police Service (SAPS) and the National Prosecuting Authority are essential to deal with, what seems to be, a serial fraudster or trafficker of babies," said Nel.

PPU SPOKESPERSON, BARRY Bateman says Van den Berg preyed on the vulnerability of men and women who yearned to be called mom and dad. "It is alleged that the prospective parents' were shown pictures of a child they hoped and prayed they would one day adopt, meanwhile the same child was promised to another couple, who were shown the same pictures, and who eventually adopted that child."

Bateman says it is alleged that in at least one instance, Van den Berg told a couple that the biological mother and child died during childbirth. "Would-be parents would prepare bedrooms and buy clothes for their adoptive children, only to be let down by Van den Berg with lies and further deception. This unbelievable cruelty earned Van den Berg hundreds of thousands of rand in fees."

The PPU thanked the police and the National Prosecuting Authority for giving the case the attention it deserves. The unit will continue to monitor developments to ensure justice is served.

Illegal adoption accused frustrates magistrate
Source: www.thepost.co.za
Publication date: 20 March 2013
Illegal adoption accused frustrates magistrate
March 20 2013 at 03:24pm
By Tania Broughton
Comment on this story

Independent Newspapers

Durban - The former owner of a Durban North children's shelter, on charges of facilitating illegal adoptions, had the justice system "over a barrel", a magistrate remarked on Tuesday.

Durban regional court magistrate Trevor Levitt was supposed to preside over the two-week trial of Hester Elizabeth van Schalkwyk.

But, in spite of the witnesses being present and the court having a clear diary, the case could not continue because Van Schalkwyk handed in doctors' certificates claiming she had had a knee operation last week and now needed treatment for a heart condition and a blood transfusion.

She had also not been able to pay her lawyers because she had been "recently widowed" and was fighting to keep her home.

On top of this, she told Levitt yesterday, she was no longer happy with her attorney and wanted to hire a new one.

"You have got this court over a barrel... I reluctantly have to agree to an adjournment because, should we run this trial and you are convicted, you will appeal and we do not want a technicality to interfere with the administration of justice," the magistrate said.

Van Schalkwyk limped into court on crutches after being ordered to appear yesterday morning when she failed to appear on Monday.

The magistrate said he had been told Van Schalkwyk had come to court the previous week to hand in a medical certificate but "at first blush" he was not satisfied that she could not attend court and sit through her trial.

And then yesterday morning, she arrived with a further certificate about treatment for a heart condition and a blood transfusion and a letter "in which she expressed concern that her relationship with her attorney (Ramond) Samuel had broken down".

The magistrate also questioned her erstwhile advocate Paul Jorgensen about why he had put on record a year ago that a trial date could be set because funds were available to pay him.

Jorgensen said his briefing attorney had given him such an assurance.

"So such an assurance is worthless?" the magistrate asked, a suggestion with which Jorgensen agreed, saying that he could not take funds directly from a client.

Van Schalkwyk, who at previous court appearances claimed to be recovering from major surgery, suffering from anaemia, hypertension and depression, undertook that at her next court appearance she would have her new attorney in tow and money would be available to engage Jorgensen again.

She will appear in court again on May 2 when a new trial date should be set.

Van Schalkwyk, who ran the Survivors' Sanctuary in Durban North, was arrested after a Carte Blanche report in which it was alleged she had tried to sell a brother and sister to several couples in 2011.

The home was subsequently shut down by the social welfare department and the children were placed in care.

She is on bail of R5 000.

The Mercury

What bothers me on the previous report is that the woman gets R5000 bail. She almost destroyed children's lives out of greed but she gets n mere R5000 bail.

In the next case the people who is supposed to look at the best interest of people was the perpetrator. The worst part is after the fact only then the organisations looked into the validation of the registrations.

Social Worker Busted For Selling Babies

Document type: News paper article

Source: www.newstime.co.za[1]

Publication date: 4 April 2011

Social Worker Busted For Selling Babies

---

1.   http://www.newstime.co.za

Monday, April 04, 2011 | Comments: 3

Social worker Sharon Mushokabanji has been busted for selling orphaned children for adoption, reports Jacques Pauw for the City Press.

Mushokabanji has since been dismissed for fraud after it emerged that she had faked her qualifications and registration with the Council for Social Service Professions. She was found by her employer, Child Welfare, to have charged illegal "adoption fees" ranging between R400 and R6,000.

City Press reports that it has obtained paperwork verifying the fraud and that police have launched an investigation into a potential child-trafficking and adoption syndicate. Mushokabanji has denied the charges and even alleged to have information on Child Welfare that she offered the City Press in return for them suppressing the story.

She also alleged that she had been receiving threats since the story broke.

Now this is what I'm talking about in fabrications of evidence.

Safe in dad's arms again

Document type: News paper article

Source: www.iol.co.za[2]

Publication date: 11 December 2008

Safe in dad's arms again

By Karyn Maughan

Falsely accused of being an abusive and mentally unstable drug addict, Jose

Williams nearly lost his baby daughter to an adoption to which he was fiercely

Opposed.

But the 26-year-old refused to give up on his first-born child and, after the claims

Made against him by his baby's mother and the Abba Adoption agency were shown

To be baseless, he won his nearly nine-month-long battle to obtain custody of the

Little girl on Wednesday.

On Wednesday, he and his daughter played "aeroplanes" together in the garden of

The family home. He grinned with delight, and she chuckled as he swung her around.

Earlier in the day, in an apparent about-turn, Abba – which had earlier wrongly

Branded Williams as an aggressive man who abused his baby's mother and had

argued that his daughter should be put up for adoption - recommended to the

Pretoria Children's Court that he be given custody.

---

2.   http://www.iol.co.za

The Children's Court agreed and awarded Williams custody for a two-year period,

during which he will apply for permanent custody of his daughter in the Pretoria High

Court.

Williams, who is preparing to lodge a complaint of unethical and unprofessional

conduct against Abba with the SA Council for Social Service Professions, now

wants to ensure that no parent ever has to "go through what I did".

Speaking to The Star at the Kensington, Joburg, home that he shares with his

mother and sisters, Williams sat with his eight-and-a-half-month-old daughter

nestled in his lap. The little girl regularly fixed her gaze on her father - who shares

her birthday with her - and beamed.

In the month since her father was allowed to remove her from the state baby home

where she spent the first seven months of her life, the little girl has gained 2kg.

"It scares me so much that I could have lost her," Williams said.

"If I hadn't been able to raise money for a lawyer and had the loving and supportive

family that I do, I don't know what would have happened. My daughter could be

living with a family on the other side of the world. I thank God that she is here with

me." Williams' ordeal began two months before his daughter was born, when the child's

mother approached Abba and asked them to arrange for the adoption.

According to the baby's mother, this was because the agency had helped her when

she fell pregnant at 17, and she wanted them to arrange that the same couple who

adopted her previous baby be given Williams' child.

But Williams was adamant that he would never give up his daughter - and it was

then that his troubles began.

Williams is now hoping that his planned complaint to the council will shed light on his

daughter's foiled adoption and expose the allegedly unlawful conduct that nearly saw it succeed.

His complaints against Abba include the following:

Under the new Children's Act, an unmarried father can acquire full parental

responsibilities and rights if he consents to be identified as the child's father or has

contributed to the child's upbringing or maintenance. All of these conditions apply to

Williams.

While Abba manager Katinka Pieterse earlier insisted to The Star that the

adoption of Williams' daughter was immediately halted when he indicated that he

opposed it, Williams insists that Abba social worker Leoni Greyling informed him

there was "nothing I could do" to stop the process.

Records from Steve Biko (formerly Pretoria) Academic Hospital reveal that

Greyling used a "Form 4" document to take Williams' daughter and place her in a place of safety affiliated with Abba after her birth. In the document, Greyling

claimed she would obtain Williams' consent for the removal. She never did.

Williams and his mother, Heloise Sequeira, learnt of his daughter's birth a week

after it happened, when Greyling sent them an SMS. They later drove to the

Pretoria Children's Court, where Sequeira said she discovered the April 16 court roll

and found a reference to her granddaughter's hearing as an inter-country adoption.

Pieterse insists that the hearing was a "child in need of care" case.

On the day of a crucial June 17 hearing into his daughter's future, Williams

Claims he received a phone call from Greyling in which she told him that he was not

Required to attend because it was "final" that the child would be adopted. She later

Wrote in a report that Williams had failed to show up at the meeting.

In another report, Greyling stated without any proof that it was "clear that the

Biological father did abuse the biological mother before and during her pregnancy".

Williams' lawyer has obtained proof that Pieterse responded to international

Queries about The Star's article on Williams' plight by claiming that Williams was a

Drug addict. Drug test results obtained by Williams – and seen by The Star – show

That he does not use drugs. Pieterse said she does not recall sending the e-mail.

Backed by SMS evidence, Williams also claims he was denied the right to visit

His daughter over a two-month period.

In response to e-mail queries from The Star, Pieterse denied any wrongdoing on

Abba's part, insisting that all issues related to Williams' daughter had been dealt

With in a legally correct way.

Danish Report Underscores 'Systematic Illegal Behavior' in South Korean Adoptions

Document type: Web page copy

Source: www.voanews.com[3]

Publication date: 28 January 2024

COPENHAGEN, DENMARK —

A Danish report on Thursday said adoptions of children from South Korea to Denmark in the 1970s and 1980s was "characterized by systematic illegal behavior" in the Asian country.

These violations, the report said, made it "possible to change information about a child's background and adopt a child without the knowledge of the biological parents."

The report was the latest in a dark chapter of international adoptions. In 2013, the government in Seoul started requiring foreign adoptions to go through family courts. The move ended the decades long policy of allowing private agencies to dictate child relinquishments, transfer of custodies and emigration.

The Danish Appeals Board, which supervises international adoptions, said there was "an unfortunate incentive structure where large sums of money were transferred between the Danish and South Korean organizations" over the adoptions.

3.　　　http://www.voanews.com

The 129-page report, published by an agency under Denmark's ministry of social affairs, focused on the period from January 1, 1970, to December 31, 1989.

A total of 7,220 adoptions were carried out from South Korea to Denmark during the two decades.

The report based its findings on 60 cases from the three privately run agencies in Denmark — DanAdopt, AC Boernehjaelp and Terres des Hommes — that handled adoptions from South Korea. The first two merged to become Danish International Adoption while the third agency closed its adoptions in 1999.

The agency wrote that two of the agencies — DanAdopt and AC Boernehjaelp — "were aware of this practice" of changing information about the child's background.

The report was made after a number of issues raised by the organization Danish Korean Rights Group. In 2022, Peter Møller, the head of the rights group, also submitted documents at the Truth and Reconciliation Commission in Seoul.

"Danish organizations continuously expressed a desire to maintain a high number of adoptions of children with a specific age and health profile from South Korea," the report said. The South Korean agencies that sent kids to Denmark were Holt Children's Services and the Korea Social Service.

The two South Korean agencies and that country's Ministry of Health and Welfare, the main government agency that handles adoption, did not immediately respond to requests for comment.

Boonyoung Han of the Danish activist group, told The Associated Press that an independent investigation was still needed because with such a probe "we expect that those responsible will finally be held accountable for their actions."

In the late 1970s and mid-1980s, South Korean agencies aggressively solicited newborns or young children from hospitals and orphanages, often in exchange for payments, and operated maternity homes where single mothers were pressured to give away their babies. Adoption workers toured factory areas and low-income neighbourhoods in search of struggling families who could be persuaded to give away their children.

On January 16, Denmark's only overseas adoption agency DIA said that it was "winding down" its facilitation of international adoptions after a government agency raised concerns over fabricated documents and procedures that obscured children's biological origins abroad. In recent years, DIA had mediated adoptions in the Philippines, India, South Africa, Thailand, Taiwan and the Czech Republic.

For years, adoptees in Europe, the United States and Australia have raised alarms about fraud, including babies who were falsely registered as abandoned orphans when they had living relatives in their native countries.

Countries: United States of America, South Africa, India, Philippines, Thailand, South Korea, Taiwan, Denmark, Czech Republic, Australia

Organizations: Danadopt (Danish Society for International child care), Holt Korea – Holt Children's Services Inc, Korea Social Service (KSS), Terre des Hommes Denmark, European Union

In South Africa 578 minor children are registered on the list for adoptable children. Many children are however caught up in the legal / social care system for years. 10 Nov 2023

Adoptions through a private social worker or adoption organisation can cost anything up to R60 000. 18 Apr 2024

While they gain their new family, an adopted child loses the experience of being raised by their biological family. Adoptees who have a closed adoption or have a very limited relationship with their birth parents can struggle with their self-esteem, a sense of loss or grief and other negative feelings.

CCA and section 243(3) of the CA, parents can apply for the rescission of the adoption order if the order was granted without their consent as required

Consent from the biological parents and / or other parties involved in the adoption can be withdrawn up to 60 days after the giving of legal consent.

By paying this huge amounts of fees to adopt children opens the door to trafficking and illegal removals.

Looking at the following statistics is this forced adoptions, paid adoptions and illegal adoptions really in the best interest of our children?

CAPE TOWN - Missing Children South Africa says more 1,300 cases of kidnapping are reported to police in the country every month.

The organisation put the spotlight on kidnapping and missing persons following the recent disappearance of six-year-old Joshlin Smith in Saldanha Bay.

Joshlin has been missing for 15 days after disappearing from her family home in Middelpos on Monday the 19th February.

Missing children SA Coordinator Bianca Van Aswegen says the high kidnapping rate and the fact that South Africa has been declared a human trafficking hub, is a huge concern.

This brings severe concerns if I think that a child, baby can be brought legally thru social services. This is a human that gets sold to the highest bidder.

To make things even worse is the fact that false birth certificates and passports for this children can easily be obtained. Like in one of the cases I recently worked on. The child was removed by social services from her mother at the age of 6 months old. Placed in Foster care with Foster parents. The social worker asked the mother to sign documents giving the foster parents permission to obtain a passport for her child, because they want to go on holiday in Germany and take her daughter with. The biological mother refused to sign the documents for a passport. With the assistance of the social worker the foster parents got a false birth certificate changing the surname of the aforesaid child to their own surname as well as a passport. They enrolled the child in school with her false birth certificate and they go abroad with the false passport.

The biological mother is denied any visitation to the child and is no contact for the past six or seven years. The child does not know her real identity and neither does she know she has another mother. Her whole life is based on fraud and lies and deception. Currently the child is twelve years old.

Not just was this child stripped of her identity, she was denied contact and bonding with her biological parent by parental alienation. Two crimes can be seen clearly in this case. Fraud, and the right to parental care.

In another case child of four years old gets taken by social services and police officials from the care of his biological mother. No reasons or prior investigations was done. The child gets placed in the custody of the biological father. But here is the problems with this case:

1. No prior investigation before removal

2. Five months after removal the first home visit gets done by social services

3. The court order states foster care placement but the child is in the father's care with a section 150 in need of care and protection.

4. At the bottom of this court order its stated that the child was removed with a detention order. A detention order is only used if a minor clashes with the law and needs to be placed in a secure environment. A child of four years old lacks criminal capacity and therefore can not be removed

from parental care with a detention order. Witch makes this court order invalid.

One of South Africa's children's Advocates made the following plea to the Government:

"Various countries refuse to adopt children from South Africa because the records were not available or destroyed by the adoption social workers.

The children who were adopted need to know who their biological parents are.

3 years ago an attorney from Pretoria had to obtain the services of a private investigators firm to track and trace the biological parents of two children who were cared for by the attorney and her own family.

This was necessary because the Christian social council social workers told the two children they have no family history.

We know that the CMR or CSC are destroying all records when they give children to adoption parents.

Letitia van den Bergh a CMR social worker doing international adoptions has been taken to the High Court when 39 couple who wanted to adopt a baby were scammed out of their money,

Letitia van den Bergh pretended to give one baby to more than a hundred parents. She did not pay the couples money back who did not receive a baby as she pretended.

This unlawful process must be stopped immediately.

We are begging Parliament Portfolio Committee to update themselves about what is going on in South Africa. The CMR or CSC social workers have illegally removed more than 200 000 children the past decade from biological parents who have a little to less money to be declared as rich people.

None of these children were abused in any way and the Department of Social Development paid the social workers to remove these children from their parents

We are a group of human rights activists who are standing for the children who have become Victims of these unlawful procedures.

Thank you for your attention"

This was a letter send to various stakeholders and departments as well as the local government. For years now child and human rights activists do petitions and letters to various institutions, numerous meetings and emails was send to the Department of Social Development. Yet we do not see any positive change.

From a anonymous source who has a registered CYCC in Pretoria they had a meeting at the Department of Social Development about baby savers. The person who is in this department and responsible for registrations of all facilities made a shocking statement. She told the owner of the CYCC. "You must stop to try and save children in need, if their parents wants to kill them or hit them it will be on their conscious not ours. My heart hardened a long time ago for children in need." Now this is a person responsible to make sure children are safe! Now how can this be OK?

This same person at the Department of Social Development was notified of a unregistered place of safety in Pretoria North and of child abuse, exploitation and child labour within this place. Numerous emails was send about this with statements from different children who was placed in that place care, this emails was send in 2022. Yet it took this Department of Social Development until 2024 to just go ahead and register this place of safety knowing of the mal practice and abuse. In addition there was even psychological assessments on some children that showed this place abuse children. But the Department of Social Development ignored all evidence and registered this place.

This is also the same place who spoke to children and told them their parents don't live or care for them and that they will adopt them. Court orders for children to be placed in this place of safety was never made out to place the children directly into this place care, the children was placed in the care of one of the workers residing on this premises. This was done because of a loophole in the legislation where a foster parent can have 6 children in her care without being registered. This means if ten workers resided at this address sixty children could be homed there without being registered. But if this children was placed under the name of this safe care the safe care would have to be registered at the Department of Social Development which they weren't.

News

DEPARTMENT OF SOCIAL DEVELOPMENT REQUESTED TO HAVE A POLICY POSITION ON INTER-COUNTRY ADOPTIONS

DSD NewsAugust 30, 2024035

The Department of Social Development in South Africa has been tasked by Parliament to establish a national policy on intercountry adoptions, as several countries are reconsidering their engagement with the programme.

Countries like the Netherlands, Norway, and Denmark have already signalled their intent to withdraw or reassess their participation in intercountry adoptions with South Africa, due to concerns about potential irregularities and ethical issues.

Since the legalisation of intercountry adoptions in 2000, South Africa has been guided by the Hague Convention's principles. However, with emerging challenges and international trends, Parliament is also pushing for a clear policy on baby savers and the rights of unmarried fathers.

The Department of Social Development has been requested by Parliament to develop a national position on intercountry adoptions. This follows recent moves by several countries to reconsider or discontinue such programmes.

The Netherlands has announced its intention to phase out intercountry adoptions with South Africa, with an official update expected next month. Norway has already ceased working with South Africa, while Sweden is set to visit in October to discuss its position. The Department also anticipates a possible withdrawal by France, following the departure of the previous Head of Central Authority. Denmark, too, is considering its withdrawal, although this has not been finalised.

This trend is not unique to South Africa; other countries are facing similar challenges. Many adoptees have discovered inaccuracies in records or evidence of illegal adoptions, which has prevented them from finding answers about their origins and identities. There is a growing acknowledgment that during the history of intercountry adoption, serious structural abuses have occurred, with some countries and intermediaries having been aware of these issues since the 1960s.

As a result, there is a noticeable decline in interest from countries in pursuing intercountry adoptions.

History of Intercountry Adoptions

Before the year 2000, South Africa did not permit intercountry adoptions. Section 18(4)(f) of the Child Care Act prohibited the adoption of South African children by non-South African citizens.

This changed following the case of Minister of Welfare & Population Development vs Fitzpatrick, where the Constitutional Court found Section 18(4)(f) of the Child Care Act unconstitutional, as it did not allow for the fulfilment of the "best interests of the child" principle. As a result, intercountry adoptions began in 2000 when the Constitutional Court's order came into effect.

South Africa then acceded to the Hague Convention on the Protection of Children and Co-operation in Respect of Intercountry Adoption (29 May 1993). In December 2003, the Convention was used to draft Chapter 16 of the Children's Act 38 of 2005.

The Convention includes basic principles that require countries to:

Establish a Central Authority to regulate intercountry adoptions,

Implement structures to prevent child trafficking,

Develop a system for accrediting child protection organisations (CPOs),

Prevent inappropriate financial gain, and

Ensure the recognition of adoption orders in both countries.

The purpose of the chapter on intercountry adoptions was to give effect to The Hague Convention, provide for the recognition of certain foreign adoptions, find fit and proper prospective adoptive parents for adoptable children, regulate intercountry adoptions, and promote and facilitate international co-operation between countries regarding intercountry adoptions.

Looking Ahead

Parliament has also requested the Department of Social Development to develop policy positions on baby savers and the traditional aspects of parental rights and responsibilities for unmarried fathers. This indicates a broader scope of review beyond just intercountry adoptions, reflecting a comprehensive approach to child welfare and protection in South Africa.

WHO COULD HAVE FAMILY care instead. This is particularly true for special needs children. Disturbingly, **one in four children with disabilities is orphaned**[4] and the percentage of children with disabilities in institutional care is three times the South African norm (**almost 30% versus the 11% of the population as a whole**[5]).

And not all facilities are as excellent as the one where Tumelo spent the last few years of his life. After the Life Esidimeni scandal, we might assume that there has been massive reform in the institutional care of adults and children with disabilities. But, if so, it has been isolated and there are still accounts of horrific abuses, particularly against non-verbal children who cannot protest or tell their stories.

It was in institutional care that twins with cerebral palsy were found shortly before they starved to death. They had each lost a third of their body weight while in the institution. Another cerebral palsy child in care was left with a brain bleed after being whipped with a cable. When he was found, he was starving, covered in bites, with faeces caked into his hands. He was so over-medicated that had his mother not discovered him when she did, he would probably have died in his sleep. And it was in an institution that a profoundly disabled teenager lost all the skin on his feet and his toenails after being lowered into scalding water.

Although some disabled children have families who could care for them with the proper support, the majority who don't need options for permanent family care. But for this to occur, the government must remain receptive to intercountry adoptions and social workers need to declare these children adoptable.

Older children too are notoriously difficult to place in national adoptions. Gelo* is eight. In a country where adoption failures are a rarity, she has had two that have left her bereft. She has no biological family to raise her and now, despite how little she is, her social workers have said they won't continue trying to place her nationally

---

4. http://www.women.gov.za/images/SITAN-Disability-Exec-Summary-low-res.pdf

5. http://www.women.gov.za/images/SITAN-Disability-Exec-Summary-low-res.pdf

because she is too old, and that intercountry adoption is not an option. Instead, they are recommending institutional care for the rest of her childhood.

Why should innocent children like Gelo grow up without a family because a government has chosen a political gesture rather than bringing criminal charges against those guilty of atrocities against adoptees? Is the preservation of her identity as a South African more important than being part of a family (she can't preserve her cultural or family heritage because she was abandoned)? Do institutions preserve culture, and if so, is that compensation for cognitive and emotional developmental delays and potential attachment problems?

Above all, is the South African government correct that it is better for her to grow up in an institution locally, rather than in another country?

If Tumelo's story has taught us anything, it's that even the best institutions can't replace family care for vulnerable children. It is too late for Tumelo to speak for himself, but if he could he may say that we need a new definition of what is in "children's best interests". **DM**

Name changed for the child's protection.
First published in the **Daily Maverick**[6]: 01.04.2021

ILLEGAL AND FORCED adoptions as well as child trafficking and illegal removals of children by social services is not limited to South Africa. This is a worldwide problem, and should not be seen as a one country issue.

---

6.   https://www.dailymaverick.co.za/opinionista/2021-04-01-are-intercountry-adoptions-in-childrens-best-interests/

Chapter 6 Organ Harvesting

The Exodus Road
     Menu
Human Trafficking Education
Organ Trafficking Facts
By Susan MaginnJanuary 16, 2023

Organ trafficking, or as it's also known, Trafficking in Persons for Organ Removal, happens around the world, as evidenced by a ring recently discovered by the Pakistani police. Worldwide this is a USD $1.7 billion industry. Learn the facts about organ trafficking.

What is organ trafficking?

When a patient suffers from organ failure and all medical interventions have been explored, an organ transplant can be the only way to stay alive. This initiates a search for a compatible organ donor. Living donors are often family members or close friends. Organ donation can also come from a deceased person who has left documented consent to be an organ donor. In the process of such ethical organ donation, no one profits financially from the organ donation.

But the current global need for organs is far greater than the supply, according to Global Observatory on Donation and Transplantation, 2020. More than 150,000 transplants are performed annually worldwide, however, this is less than 10% of the global need. Some sick patients are willing to break the law and pay for an organ transplant, even if it involves exploiting vulnerable and impoverished people.

The terms "Organ Trafficking" and "Trafficking in Persons for Organ Removal" actually represent two very different crimes with distinct legal implications. "Organ Trafficking" refers to the illegal handling of organs. For example, selling an organ for profit or advertising the willingness to buy or sell an organ is organ trafficking.

"Trafficking in Persons for Organ Removal" is when a person of vulnerability is exploited, deceived, coerced, or abused for the illicit use of their organ. The organ doesn't even have to be removed for this crime to take place, since it is the trafficking of the person that is the crime.

How prevalent is organ trafficking?

The organ trade, which includes illegal organ transplants, generates significant income, with conservative annual estimates between USD $840 million to USD $1.7 billion and 12,000 illegal transplants. About 10% of all transplants are believed to be illegal transplants.

Organ trafficking is far less common than labor or sex trafficking, partly because of the high level of medical knowledge and coordination necessary for the crime to take place. However, experts state that the magnitude of the problem is difficult to track since the crimes often happen within a network of legitimate medical settings with legally certified medical professionals.

"While trafficking in human beings for organ removal is not a new phenomenon, it is underreported due to the clandestine nature of the crime, combined with a lack of awareness by law enforcement agencies and the deficiency of information sharing channels between the medical and police sectors," said Cyril Gout, INTERPOL's Direct of Operational Support and Analysis.

We are just beginning to understand the scope of this crime as illustrated by the fact that the United States Department of Justice does not even include organ removal in its definition of human trafficking.

The Exodus Road

Menu

Human Trafficking Education

Organ Trafficking Facts

By Susan MaginnJanuary 16, 2023

Organ trafficking, or as it's also known, Trafficking in Persons for Organ Removal, happens around the world, as evidenced by a ring recently discovered by the Pakistani police. Worldwide this is a USD $1.7 billion industry. Learn the facts about organ trafficking.

What is organ trafficking?

When a patient suffers from organ failure and all medical interventions have been explored, an organ transplant can be the only way to stay alive. This initiates a search for a compatible organ donor. Living donors are often family members or close friends. Organ donation can also come from a deceased person who has left documented consent to be an organ donor. In the process of such ethical organ donation, no one profits financially from the organ donation.

But the current global need for organs is far greater than the supply, according to Global Observatory on Donation and Transplantation, 2020. More than 150,000 transplants are performed annually worldwide, however, this is less than 10% of the global need. Some sick patients are willing to break the law and pay for an organ transplant, even if it involves exploiting vulnerable and impoverished people.

The terms "Organ Trafficking" and "Trafficking In Persons for Organ Removal" actually represent two very different crimes with distinct legal implications. "Organ Trafficking" refers to the illegal handling of organs. For example, selling an organ for profit or advertising the willingness to buy or sell an organ is organ trafficking.

"Trafficking in Persons for Organ Removal" is when a person of vulnerability is exploited, deceived, coerced, or abused for the illicit use of their organ. The organ doesn't even have to be removed for this crime to take place, since it is the trafficking of the person that is the crime.

How prevalent is organ trafficking?

The organ trade, which includes illegal organ transplants, generates significant income, with conservative annual estimates between USD $840 million to USD $1.7 billion and 12,000 illegal transplants. About 10% of all transplants are believed to be illegal transplants.

Organ trafficking is far less common than labor or sex trafficking, partly because of the high level of medical knowledge and coordination necessary for the crime to take place. However, experts state that the magnitude of the problem is difficult to track since the crimes often happen within a network of legitimate medical settings with legally certified medical professionals.

"While trafficking in human beings for organ removal is not a new phenomenon, it is underreported due to the clandestine nature of the crime, combined with a lack of awareness by law enforcement agencies and the deficiency of information sharing channels between the medical and police sectors," said Cyril Gout, INTERPOL's Direct of Operational Support and Analysis.

We are just beginning to understand the scope of this crime as illustrated by the fact that the United States Department of Justice does not even include organ removal in its definition of human trafficking.

Young woman wearing a mask riding a public bus

What organs are most frequently trafficked?

Kidneys are the most common on the "organ market," followed by livers and corneas. Emerging markets exist for human eggs, skin, human embryos, and blood plasma.

Where does organ trafficking occur?

Trafficking in Persons for Organ Removal happens all around the world, but the highest numbers are in Northern Africa and in the Middle East. It is also more common in South and South-East Asia, Central America and Europe. When someone is willing to travel abroad for the purpose of obtaining an organ it is called Transplant Tourism.

Transplant tourism often happens in countries where there are fewer regulations. This is how traffickers can build criminal networks with the coordination of corrupt medical professionals, hospital administrators, laboratory staff, drivers, translators, and law enforcement.

Who are the most common victims of Trafficking in Persons for Organ Removal?

Refugees, migrants, and asylum seekers are targets of traffickers as they may be desperate to provide for themselves and their families in their host country and willing to use an organ to pay a smuggler's fee. According to the United Nations Office on Drugs and Crime (UNODC), the average victim is a young adult male, around 30 years old.

How are victims of organ trafficking recruited?

Donors are recruited online and in person. They are usually people who are vulnerable due to a lack of financial stability. They may be uneducated and told lies by traffickers that kidneys grow back, that they have three kidneys, or that they will be given medical care after the surgery. They are promised anywhere from $500 to $10,000 but may never be paid at all. They are sometimes forced to sign papers indicating valid consent or to declare that they are related to the patient.

In the case in Pakistan in January 2023, the victims were lured with promises of jobs and large payouts. Their kidneys were sold for up to the equivalent of USD $4,000.

Unfortunately, victims of Trafficking in Persons for Organ Removal can sometimes be mistaken as criminals because they are being paid. However, we need to consider what exactly makes someone a victim of human trafficking and what makes them a criminal. A victim of human trafficking is someone who is recruited, deceived, harbored, transported, coerced, and exploited.

One might think that if someone is paid for their organ, then they are profiting and therefore a part of the crime and not a victim of human trafficking, but if a donor was coerced and their vulnerability exploited, it would not be considered valid consent. The World Health Organization, among other authorities, actually requires a psychological evaluation to confirm that the donor is not financially profiting from or otherwise coerced into organ donation.

What can be done about organ trafficking?

Awareness-raising campaigns can make a difference to educate the general public and increase accountability among medical professionals. However, tracking the scale of the problem remains complicated. While other forms of human trafficking for sex or forced labor generally happen repeatedly over a period of time, human trafficking for organ removal only happens once, making it more difficult to track.

Those who have been trafficked for organ removal may remain silent because selling an organ has a stigma and is illegal. Therefore, the very person who has been exploited might fear being charged as a criminal. Confidentiality and patient privacy, while an essential component of professional medical care, can actually hinder legal investigations.

In October 2022, the (UNODC) released a toolkit to support the investigation and prosecution of this crime. This toolkit is a big step forward in the international community to build the capacity of law enforcement to address this crime.

Many victims of forced organ harvesting have previously been exploited through human trafficking and other forms of slavery. Other victims are murdered on demand and have their organs removed to fulfil an order.

Illegal organ trafficking is growing across Africa. The sophisticated operation is worth over $1 billion annually and targets the vulnerable. Lack of regulation and huge demand for organs drive the trade.

Illegal (e.g., Iran is the only country in the world where buying and selling an organ is legal but this exception only applies to its citizens). Conversely, there are few laws that restrict an individual from leaving one's country to obtain an organ from someone abroad. In fact, there are many companies that cater to "transplant tourism" but purport to only match up recipients with donors who are willing.

How do these traffickers operate?

Traffickers typically operate within complex and elusive global networks, requiring a sophisticated infrastructure involving medical specialists, logistical coordination and access to healthcare facilities. They connect with their victims using local advertisements, social media or via direct approaches by recruiters, who may be former victims themselves or trusted individuals within the victim's community.

These criminal networks are highly organized and flexible, often functioning as mobile units or specialized groups. Key players include brokers who coordinate logistics, recruit medical professionals, and prepare fraudulent documents. To ensure smooth operations, they rely on a wide range of facilitators such as healthcare officials, hospital administrators, customs officers and local recruiters.

Detecting this crime can be challenging, as traffickers often train victims to pretend that they are related to the recipient to evade suspicion during evaluations at hospitals or clinics.

How do illicit organ transplants affect victims?

The long-term health consequences for victims can be devastating, with many experiencing a sharp decline in their physical condition post-surgery, along with stigmatization and depression. The psychological impacts often lead to a further deterioration in their standard of living, trapping them in a cycle of poverty and poor health.

Dal involving the sale and transplantation of kidneys on three continents.

The donors were mostly poor Brazilians willing to sell a kidney for up to $10 000 (£5400; €8000) each. The recipients were Israelis who paid up to 10 times that amount for a kidney.

A senior nephrologist, Dr Jeff Kallmeyer, is on trial in Durban facing charges under the Human Tissues Act. South African law forbids the sale of organs for transplantation and requires the establishment of some relationship between donor and recipient for privately arranged transplantations. Accordingly, it is alleged that the Brazilian donors and Israeli recipients had to sign fraudulent documents stating they were related. Several other surgeons and medical staff have also been arrested and are facing trial.

The main financial beneficiaries, however, seem to have been the intermediaries who organised the transplantations, matching donors and recipients and arranging the logistics in South Africa.

South African investigators have frozen the assets of one of these men—an Israeli living in South Africa who is said to be key to the South African operation—while he is tried in Durban.

Most of the transplantations, said to number in the hundreds, are alleged to have taken place in two hospitals owned by the Netcare group, with most done at St Augustine's Hospital in Durban. Reports from other countries indicate that donors and recipients may have come from other countries as well, with all operations taking place in South Africa.

Netcare, which provides services on contract to the NHS in Britain, has consistently denied any wrongdoing throughout the investigation.

According to US press reports, Israel has a shortage of donors, as religious Jews seldom donate organs, claiming that their religion forbids it.

As the investigators arrested participants in the scheme, several of the poorer Brazilian donors found themselves not only without a kidney but without payment when they got back to Brazil.

It is alleged that when the scheme was running, donors had their passports confiscated on arrival in South Africa, and were provided with a low standard of hotel accommodation.

https://www.ncbi.nlm.nih.gov/pmc/articles/PMC487760/

The socioeconomic impact of the COVID-19 pandemic is expected to fuel Trafficking in persons for the purpose of organ removal (THBOR -is one of the most coercive, exploitative forms of the human organ trade) as it will likely be easier for brokers to coerce vulnerable individuals to sell an organ to improve their economic conditions. This is exacerbated by the fact that legal organ donations, and therefore transplants, have suffered major decreases since the outbreak of COVID-19"

Then currently, the Russian invasion of Ukraine has plundered the people there into total desperation in every aspect and many are becoming refugees which worstens the situation and because of the desperations presented they are now vulnerable to predators who will exploit their vulnerabilities to recruit victims into all forms of trafficking.

Live donations should occur with the donor's informed and voluntary consent and that donors should be provided professional medical care (Guiding Principle 3),

• cells, tissues, and organs should be donated, not sold, and that sales should be prohibited, though compensation for donations is permitted (Guiding Principle 5), and

• health professionals should not engage in, or provide insurance coverage for, transplantations that involved "exploitation or coercion of, or payment.

The following was in IOL online News and shows what is happening in South Africa.

Published Apr 9, 2017

By Nabeelah Shaikh

| Published Apr 9, 2017

Human organs for sale were advertised on the side of the road in Cape Town this week.

According to pamphlets distributed by the New Day Clinic, you can get the body part you want within a week, with the transplants being done at their world-class medical facility.

A price list for organs – including kidneys, livers, hearts, guts and veins – were displayed on the clinic's website.

It claimed you can buy a kidney for just over R3.5million, while a patch of skin will set you back R140 per square centimetre. Eyes are sold for just R2000 each, while a second-hand spleen will cost R7 000. A shocked motorist reported that a "Nigerian woman" dressed in a surgical mask and white latex gloves handed out the pamphlets. Sounds like a script from a movie? It is.The dark world of Illegal organ trading will be highlighted in Africa's first medical thriller movie called Bypass, set to hit cinemas early next month.

The movie stars local actors Natalie Becker-Aakervik, Hakeem-Kae Kazim, Deon Lotz and Greg Kriek. The issue of illegal organ trade was on the lips of many South Africans after the news of the clinic selling organs in Cape Town for millions of rands hit the streets.

Pamphlets were circulated at traffic lights with information regarding the New Day Clinic, which directed people to a website with a price list for various organs.

South Africans took to social media to express shock at the website but it was part of the movie's promotional campaign – designed to draw attention to a trade that is very real.

In 2007, the World Health Organisation estimated that out of all transplants worldwide, 5%-10% were conducted illegally.

In 2011, it was estimated that the illicit organ trade generated profits between $600million (R8billion) and $1.2billion per year. Underground markets pose a significant threat to the security of national organ donation systems.

There is a long list of more than 4300 people awaiting solid organ and cornea transplants in South Africa.

This does not include the thousands of people who do not make it onto the waiting list as they don't have access to the facilities or treatment required to keep them alive while they wait.

"In the case of patients in renal failure, if they do not have access to dialysis they will not be placed on the waiting list. There are not nearly enough dialysis machines in South Africa and the result is that many patients are sent home to die," said Samantha Nicholls from the Organ Donor Association of South Africa. Less than 2% of South Africans are organ donors.

In Durban, 19-year-old Matthew Legemaate from Hillcrest is among one of the many people who are on the list. Legemaate has been waiting for a heart and a bilateral lung for six years.

Not long after his birth, Legemaate was diagnosed with Tetralogy of Fallot and severe pulmonary atresia, a congenital heart defect which has required five open-heart surgeries thus far. His only hope now is if he receives a new heart and lung. His mother, Janet, said every day was an uphill battle for Matthew and his family.

"We know what it has been like and it's every parent's worst nightmare to watch their child have to suffer throughout their lives. Matthew's case is also more complicated because he has a rare blood type.

"If you no longer need your organs in the case of death, it's an incredible gift that you can give towards changing someone's life. More people need to become organ donors because we really are suffering in South Africa," she said.

The producers of Bypass, husband and wife Shane and Bianca Vermooten, hope that those who watch it will become organ donors and contribute to the solution.

"If there were sufficient legal organs available the need for a black-market trade would decrease significantly," said Nicholls.

Their aim is for Bypass to send a clear message: organ trafficking is a frightening reality that preys on the desperation of the wealthy and the vulnerability of the poor.Shane Vermooten said he believed in the concept that "every human life was of equal worth". The movie explores a mother's love for her dying son and makes us question how far we would go to save our own child's life.

https://www.unodc.org/

Case Law Database

Trafficking in persons

Other Crimes

State v. Netcare Kwa-Zulu Limited

South Africa

Fact Summary

In November 2010, under the authority of the South African National Director of Public Prosecution, Netcare Kwa-Zulu (Pty) Limited entered into an agreement whereby it pleaded guilty to 102 counts related to charges stemming from having allowed its 'employees and facilities to be used to conduct ... illegal kidney transplant operations'. In addition to Netcare, a number of other charges were laid against the St Augustine's Hospital, located in Durban, South Africa, the CEO of Netcare, Richard Friedland, and eight others: four transplant doctors, a nephrologist, two transplant administrative coordinators, and an interpreter. The admission of guilt related to 109 illegal kidney transplant operations that took place between June 2001 and November 2003. The scheme involved Israeli citizens in need of kidney transplants who would be brought to South Africa for transplants performed at St Augustine's Hospital.

While the kidneys supplied originally came from Israeli citizens, 'later Romanian and Brazilian citizens were recruited as their kidneys were obtainable at a much lower cost'. The broker, Ilan Perry, was the individual who was in charge of the recruitment of both kidney suppliers and recipients and was not South African and has not been charged. He set a fee of between USD 100,000 and USD 120,000 for recipients and paid the original suppliers of kidneys USD 20,000. However, later on in the scheme, Romanians and Brazilians received on average of USD 6,000.

Ilan Perry used recruiters to source individuals ready to supply kidneys; two of these, Captain Ivan Da Silva and Gaby Tauber, had been imprisoned in Brazil for their roles in the affair. Blood screening of prospective kidney suppliers was done in-country and again in South Africa in an attempt to 'ensure sufficient compatibility with prospective recipients'; those deemed suitable were 'accommodated and chaperoned' and 'given documents to sign falsely indicating that they were related to each other'. This fraudulent activity was meant to circumvent the requirement to gain outside approval, via a Ministerial Committee, for transplants of unrelated principals. While Netcare Kwa-Zulu (Pty) Limited was paid up-front for its participation in the illegal kidney transplants, the people supplying the healthy kidneys were paid after the fact and in cash.

The charges to whichh Netcare Kwa-Zulu (Pty) Limited pleaded guilty were laid under the South African Human Tissue Act 1983 and the Prevention of Organised Crime Act 1998. It might be mentioned that the company escaped charges which had been leveled at the other accused, including fraud, forgery, and assault with intent to do grievous bodily harm (for operations without informed consent). The Human Tissue Act 1983 prohibited the transplantation of the tissue of minors into another living person; requiring that written consent be provided; and that no purchase of tissue, such as kidneys, was allowed. Further, there existed a Ministerial Policy of the Department of Health which set out, inter alia, that:

"Donor organs must be used primarily for South African citizens and permanent residents. Written consent must be obtained from the Minister of Health before any person who is not a South African citizen or permanent resident is accepted onto a transplantation programme."

The Ministerial policy also established that a Ministerial Committee had to approve applications for transplantation of unrelated living donors so as 'to reduce the possibility of abuse'.

The prosecutor later argued that the company and the other accused must have been aware of the law and policy regarding transplants from living donors, and that they had to try to find a way to portray ostensible compliance with the current policy and legislation. They therefore created the pretence that the kidney suppliers were related to the recipients.

The first charge—counts 1 to 5—to which Netcare Kwa-Zulu (Pty) Limited pleaded guilty related to the use of five minors as organ suppliers in violation of the Human Tissue Act 1983. The employees of St Augustine's Hospital were recognised, in the convoluted Charge Sheet of the Prosecutor, to be 'acting on behalf of the accused company and were about the exercised of their powers and the performance of their duties as employees of the company furthering or endeavouring to further the interests of the company', in carrying out these illegal kidney transplants. Counts 6 to 10 constituted the second charge and related to receiving payment for the kidney transplants emanating from the five minors. It might be mentioned that Netcare Kwa-Zulu (Pty) Limited received payments from the broker and it then disbursed payment 'to the other accused and service providers; including the surgeons for their services'. The third charge, consisting of counts 11 through 102, related to contravention of the Prevention of Organised Crime Act 1998. In regard to the 102 transplant operations that did not includee minors, the company pleaded guilty to its employees having received money, the proceeds of an unlawful activity; while Netcare Kwa-Zulu (Pty) Limited admitted that 'in the circumstances', it knew 'that the aforementioned property formed part of the proceeds of unlawful activities'.

In the Agreement between Netcare Kwa-Zulu (Pty) Limited and the State, the State recognised its own legitimate interest 'in overseeing the control over transplant of human tissues [...] the interests of the medical profession and the public at large'. Where the public interest was concerned, the Agreement noted:

"that a company, such as the accused company, guilty of an offence such as this, should be convicted and punished and more particularly, that that conviction and punishment should take place in open court for society as a whole to come to know and understand that the prosecuting authorities and the Department of Health will not tolerate breaches of the code of conduct and standards of ethics and compliance with the law required in a civilised society."

The Agreement then set out the penalty Imposed: a confiscation order of ZAR 3,800,000 (approximately USD 466,839) amounting to the benefit the company derived from the offences, plus a sentence of ZAR 4,020,000 (approximately USD 493,875) amounting to fines for each of the counts to which Netcare Kwa-Zulu (Pty) Limited pleaded guilty.

Commentary and Significant Features

The agreement, whereby Netcare Kwa-Zulu (Pty) Limited and St Augustine's Hospital admitted guilt to having knowingly allowed its employees and facilities to be used for what amounted to the trafficking of persons for their organs, constituted one of the first such cases to make its way before a court of law. In so doing, the agreement implicated and effectively prosecuted the hospital involved. The case did not add to the international jurisprudence, as South Africa was not party to the UN Trafficking in Persons Protocol when the material facts took place. However, it did speak to the legitimate inclusion of provisions dealing with the trafficking in persons for their organs within the definition of trafficking of persons found in article 3(a) the Protocol.

2020 Nov; 87(4): 372–373. Published online 2020 Aug 11. Doi: 10.1177/0024363920944841

PMCID: PMC7551533PMID: 33100383

"Death by Donation": Harvesting Organs from Still-Living Persons

Justo Aznar, MD, PhD1

Author information Copyright and License information PMC Disclaimer

An interesting and at the same time highly disturbing article published in Intensive Care Medicine (Ely 2019) discusses the procurement of organs for transplants from people who may want euthanasia or assisted suicide, and who, instead of achieving their goal via the usual procedure, agree to undergo surgery in an operating theatre to remove their organs while still alive. This has been called "death by donation," that is, these people die when their organs are removed. The issue arises due to the shortage of organs for transplant in most developed countries, resulting in long waiting lists of patients who require a transplant.

Faced with this problem, the article in question mentions "off the table" solutions for these patients, such as resorting to the "black market" in underdeveloped countries, and asking whether we would consider other options, such as obtaining them from a living person who wishes to die and who offers to donate their organs in the same surgical procedure that will bring about their death.

At various international medical conferences held in 2018–2019, many discussions centred on "donation after death", which it seems is already being practiced in countries like Canada and the Benelux countries, where euthanasia or assisted suicide are legal. According to the author, the so-called Imminent Death Donation refers to terminally-ill patients requesting euthanasia who are willing to donate their organs, while "by death donation" may include volunteers who have no illness, that is, healthy people who want to commit suicide.

The main bioethical problem Is that "death by donation" infringes upon a deeply rooted medical standard that prohibits the harvesting of organs for donation until the donor is declared dead. Thus, "death by donation" would, at present, be considered homicide for ending a human life, even if it is for a seemingly good end, namely, procuring organs for donation.

In addition to all this, and when attributing ethical responsibilities to those who participate in these acts, we must bear in mind that in euthanasia practices or in assisted suicide, the intervention of only one physician is necessary, while "death by donation" requires a full team of medical professionals. So, the question is, would the entire team of medical professionals consent to participate in this clearly homicidal medical act? Moreover, would the organ recipient also consent to receive organs from a living person who offered to die, so that their organs could be harvested?

It Is certainly another step in the mad race to end human lives because in our view, "death by donation" is a homicidal act, as is euthanasia. This is especially true if—as is attested to in another article in the New England Journal of Medicine (Chambaere et al. 2015)—of the 3,882 deaths from euthanasia or assisted suicide performed in the Netherlands and Belgium in 2013, 1,047 (27 percent) were carried out without being requested by the patients and consequently without their consent.

Where and to what extent does Organ Harvesting take place?

Organ harvesting or evidence of organ harvesting exists in various countries in the world, especially in China, India, and on the Sinai Peninsula.

People's Republic of China

Organ transplantation in the People's Republic of China is booming, with the number of transplants rising. A distribution system for donor organs as in Europe, or a culture of organ donation, does not exist. Thus, the origin of tens of thousands of organs is remains unclear.

Numerous pieces of evidence suggest that people were murdered on this scale in order to sell and transplant their organs – indeed, with the involvement and support of government agencies. Thus, the most cases of organ harvesting in the world by far take place in China.

Sinai Peninsula

According to the World Health Organization (WHO), Egypt has become a regional hub of organ trafficking. In 2010, at least 14.000 refugees were brought over the border into Israel by smuggling networks. On their way through Egypt, the refugees and migrants are frequently intercepted by organized criminals and are released only through a ransom. According to the UN Refugee Agency, if family members of the refugees cannot pay a ransom, they are sold to gangs in the northern Sinai, where they often killed and robbed of their organs.

Approximately 1,000 camps are part of the so-called "Laogai" complex. According to various estimates, the Chinese authorities exploit between three and seven million people as slaves – seven days a week, sometimes up to 18 hours a day. Torture and violence, insufficient food and water, sleep deprivation, and the denial of medical care are everyday occurrences for many prisoners.

A huge number of prisoners are detained completely arbitrarily, without having committed a crime. Chinese police departments can (without judges or lawyers) 'administratively' admit citizens of the People's Republic to forced labour camps for "re-education through labour" for up to four years – without an accusation, a court procedure and without the possibility of defence or appeal. Evidence suggests that followers of Buddhist meditation school Falun Gong who have been arbitrarily imprisoned are especially likely to become victims of organ harvesting. However, Uyghurs and other prisoners are also frequent victims of organ harvesting.

Condemned to Death

In 2005, the People's Republic of China admitted that organs of executed people are removed, even though this practice violates international law. Chinese human rights activists report that inmates on death row are forced to sign organ donation forms. According to various estimates, several thousand people are executed every year in the People's Republic – the exact number is state secret. Previously, those condemned to death were executed primarily through being shot in the head, and later often through lethal injection. Today, executions must take place at least in part through organ removal in order to ensure the quality of the organs. In the People's Republic of China, the death penalty can be imposed for a number of offenses that are not internationally considered felonies. In many cases, Chinese courts impose the death penalty based on confessions obtained under torture.

Refugees and Victims of Poverty

Refugees from Eritrea, Sudan and Ethiopia who try to reach Europe through Egypt or Israel are especially vulnerable to becoming victims of severe human rights violations in the Sinai region, including organ harvesting.

What is the evidence?

The Chinese authorities consistently block access to information and on-site inspections. Therefore, it is very difficult to obtain judicial evidence. However, there is a wealth of compelling evidence proving that people are killed for their organs on a large scale in the People's Republic of China. The reason and starting point for all research was and is the completely unclear origin of thousands of "donor" organs.

Forced organ harvesting cannot be ignored. This is an undeniably heinous practice that plagues our society, but little has been done to right these wrongs. To address such a significant ethical issue, collaborative efforts are required from citizens, physicians, activists, politicians, and international committees. Everyone has a responsibility to take action

Chapter 7 Adrenachrome

Do we know what adrenachrome is? Can we ever fully understand in order to get adrenachrome we need to produce adrenalin? What is adrenacrome used for? And how does it get produced?

I will try and explain this thru numerous illustrations and information that I found on this topic. As it's a very dark, cruel, inhumane topic there is not a lot available in resources about it. And quite frankly most places dubbed it as a conspiracy theory. But is it?

We know thru centuries that in Satanic rituals blood gets spilled and consumed. Ever wondered why this is done? What is the purpose? Some would say it's a sacrifice, true but what other benefits does the drinker get?

What even shocks me more as the author of this book is that there is actually adrenacrome factories. Real factories that produces adrenachrome and that some governments, elites and business owners is partners in this factories.

If you ever wondered why so many people especially young children suddenly has all sorts of mental illness and is placed on antipsychotic medications from a young age read this chapter with a open mind.

"DEXTER CHILDREN SAVED from E *V E R *GRE EN shipping container"

◇P.S. E V ER GREEN is H. C li n ton's nickname

"It Takes a Village - Laura Silsby and the
Clinton Foundation";
"Predictive Programming For
Normalization of Acceptance":
More Background for a better understanding as to what this pan sexual agenda is all about,... grooming our children through the schools for...
*T R A F F I C KING; https://www.facebook.com/story.php/?id=100064499387593&story_fbid=528034946023147
"E V E R G REEN IS PEOPLE" https://www.facebook.com/story.php/?id=538690142808571&story_fbid=4081483205195896
"Stuck at sea: Cargo ship wedged in Suez Canal causes traffic jam"

- Sky News

◇► https://youtu.be/FH-_Mtkugbs?si=amRA2D3lvNEeCr69
"Container Ship That Blocked the Suez Canal is Loading Containers"
◇►   https://youtube.com/shorts/gkUcaNLosyQ?si=tlbysOz3GTZZ4ra9
◇ While the house with the tunnels featured in my images may be completely sweet and innocent, there is a dark underbelly reflective of concerns for these tunnels, especially ones that are clearly built for children. What stood out as a red flag with the set up within this house featured was the reference of "Alice in Wonderland" and, the white◇ bunny. In the traff ic King circles, the white rabbit represents ◇Adrenachrome.

Something that also blaringly sticks out, some of these homes with these tunnels, shared in the last 10 photos from the featured article,...there are homes which have tunnels that open out to the ocean. One may say that some of these older tunnels could be connected to the days of prohibition, where they use them to traffic liquor, but as you can see by the article, these specific tunnels and rooms were designed for children

◈Information that came out during the Max well trials was that she had a submarine license, where it was stated that these underwater cavernous areas were developed off the shores of these privately owned islands specifically to imprison these children, where the elites would come to safely carry out their atrocities.◈

G. M a x well's submarine history :

◈ Look at this post on Facebook https://www.facebook.com/share/SYcgm3vurkWbuiQG/?mibextid=hubsqH

How many young and unfortunate lives have been buried at sea?

"Losing More than 1800 Containers, The Most Epic Large Container Ship Disaster Costs $ Billions"

- Nauctis

◈▶ https://youtu.be/yrfQ63EyEuA?si=MwIM_dpkw1QQ7bUF

"R◈ot breaks out in New York City sy nag ogue over S E C R E T T U N N E L"

The dark history behind the mystery of the tunnels and the children:

https://www.facebook.com/share/VzEiaC7zDMrerfEf/?mibextid=WC7FNe

BACKGROUND:

"Will Ferrell's "Comedy" Skit About Child Trafficking Is Absolutely Disgusting"

What the Censored and Bought-Out Media Won't Show,...

Exposing the Perversity of Justice Upon WITCH Sit The Rich and Powerful. Generations Stolen and Broken.

The Target = Our Children,...

Taking Down Paedosadists, Child Traffickers, Vaccine killers, Organ,...Adrenachrome,...Melanin smugglers? DynCorp, supplies services and training to the FBI, SEC, DEA, CIA, FAA, CDC, 60%

of U.S. Army's helicopter fleet , 80% of NASA ships, our prison system , DEA, and our police forces around the world. (I might've left out a few branches.) DynCorp is tied into the controlling powers of our leaders and elite, also connected with the ongoing child trafficking abuses around the world. The Clinton Foundation is connected with slave labour, environmental degradation and, human trafficking around the world, with one sensational case in Morna Bossa, Haiti, at their Caracol Industrial Complex, where there is a DynCorp connection with the whole set-up. Target, Gap and, Walmart are amongst other Clinton owned businesses associated. DynCorp Receives more than 96% of its more than 3 billion an annual revenues from the US federal government.

DynCorp's Sister company, DynPort Vaccine Company has been involved in the scandals Of child sex trafficking, child pornography and other criminal acts, some of which involve contaminating vaccines, purposely infecting patients with hepatitis C. If anyone has noticed, there's this new advertisement on TV touting the increase of hepatitis C and the need for more medication.

DynCorp's company controllers, Cerberus Capital Management is owned by Zionist Steve Feinberg.

The rings are connected to those in enforcement, and law where-by safely able to continue controlling and hiding their activities and, the sick facts from the public. The DynCorp connection sheds light on why the continued negligence of justice. It's near impossible to expect a parasitic system to cultivate a healthy environment. Specifics on DynCorp and how it ties into child sex trafficking are easily researched, also included in Part 3 Of a documentary shared below. This is a very informative well researched documentary I recommend viewing, for anyone interested in the subject.

"The Finders"

Result = Complicit CPS (70% of children held in care by CPS are trafficked) Removing Your Child for unhindered abuse programming,... trafficking.

This is a purposeful erosion of humanity and care within society. I have also written about an ongoing effort to eradicate the Age of Consensual sex with minors. This is spearheaded by the Vatican and associates. All of this can be easily researched.

Paedophilia is not an isolated situation rather, a carefully groomed manipulation of the innocence of society as a whole. If you pay attention, it stands out in commercials, movies and even the history of sexual education, back to Roman days where they practiced Saturnalia, which is satanic,. Involving children in sexual public orgies, which also includes (using this word in the present tense as this is still ongoing) sacrificing babies by throwing them into a fire within the effigy of their Owl God, Moloch. Paedophilia conditioning of the public continued with Dr. Sigmund Freud, who believed that all children were born with natural sexual urge towards one or both of their parents, calling it, "infant sexuality". He felt that there was a progression of oral, anal, and genital phases. Freud's son, Sir Clement Freud, has been accused of consistent accounts of child molestation and rape. This sick philosophy continues through Wilhelm Reich, who wrote the influential, "The Sexual Struggle of Youth". He claimed all people had the tendency for fascism, particularly if they were sexually repressed in their youth, which he felt was evil. The only way to stop this fascism was to of course sexualize them as children.

"Suppression of the natural sexuality in the child, particularly of its general sexuality, makes the child apprehensive, shy, obedient, afraid of authority, good and adjusted in the authoritarian sense."

- Wilhelm Reich

Ing and raping children To tearful cries, which he then marked as pleasure and orgasm. His research also included regular monitored and compensated behavior of other paedophiles,... nurturing the behavior within the community. Kinsey and his associates also testified and wrote in favour of Early parole for paedophiles and violent sex offenders, claiming their right to therapy versus retribution. Further, all of Kinsey's research was based around deviant sexual behavior from burlesque dancers, strippers, prostitutes, pimps, convicts, Paedophiles, and, homosexuals,... all which goes against the natural order. His preoccupation was impressing deviant sexuality as normal,... claiming all normal sexual behavior was deviant. To this day all violent sexual offenders and paedophiles get released back onto the street to continue to offend. His influence sparked the sexual revolution of the 60's, powerfully re-shaping sexuality,... onward becoming the sexual education textbooks within our schools. His research was funded by the Rockefeller foundation. Simultaneously in the 60s,

Hugh Hefner, a huge fan of the philosophies of Kinsey, as shared during interviews, began projecting further deviant sexual behavior into society through his magazines, showcasing not just women, but children. Along with the popularity of these came an alarming rate of deviant violence sexual crimes. This became such an issue that the Department of Justice hired Dr. Judith Reisman To research the content of Playboy, Penthouse, and, Hustler magazines, published and distributed between the 60s and 80s. Amazingly, she found 9,000 sexual scenarios with children under age 18, an average of about 8-9 images per issue! These images involving children are quite disturbing graphically and, the language used toward them. There is also extreme violence depicted towards children as well. Dr. Reisman went on to continue her research and speaking out on the growing sexual violence and paedophilia within society. Basically these magazines are grooming the masses towards paedophilic tendencies.

- The documentary is shared below.

Now through Common Core, they are not only dumbing down our kids but, also sexualizing them, beginning at age 5, starting with birth control,...by 3rd/5th grade, offering demonstrations on how to properly use sex toys. Consider the form of education,... first start them out with birth control and then, sex toys. The other large motivation for this program is to indoctrinate children to no longer gender identify but rather be open to being another gender and rather groom them to a identity with another gender other than that of their birth. Parents risk imprisonment already in some locations for not supporting the child in identifying with the opposite gender. The focus on supporting gay rights and transsexualism is not to support the actual cause but, has a much darker agenda of controlling the population and the satanic uprising of grooming generations of hermaphrodite's. That's not sexual education, that is priming,...sexualizing our children for promiscuity, deterioration of human nature, driving in the final nail in the coffin of humanity.

"I served in the Georgia state Senate and after four years of viewing the ruthless and unsparing actions of Child Protective Services, also called CPS, which I will use tonight. I wrote a scathing report about the corrupt business of Child Protective Services. The report cost me my Senate seat however, there are causes worth losing over,...and this is one.

Funding is available when a child becomes placed in a foster home with strangers or placed

In a mental health facility and medicated, usually against the parents wishes. Parents are victimized by the system that makes a profit for holding children longer and bonuses for not returning children to their parents. This is abuse of power, it is lack of accountability, and it is a growing criminal, political phenomenon, spreading around the globe. Often times but not always, poor parents are targeted to lose their children because they do not have money enough to hire an attorney or fight the system. Being poor and lacking proper housing does not mean your children should be removed. CPS has redefined poor to mean psychologically inferior therefore, it is in the best interest of the child to be removed. Best interest of course has also been re-defined, at the child's expense. It has been reported over and over that 6x as many children die in foster care than in the general public. Once a child is legally kidnapped and placed in 'official safety', the child is far more likely to suffer abuses, Including sexual molestation and or, rape."

    - Former Georgia State Senator Nancy Schaefer. She and her husband were killed after exposing CPS.

"The Future is Fluid"

Goal = End to Humanity, as a whole . Trans-genders and, gay couples can not naturally co-create life. This movement was nurtured as a satanic merging with their hermaphroditic Baphomet.

'Terminal Wokeness' = Conformity to This Abomination As Normal!?!

If we don't recognize the demons in front of us, how will they? Who will be the voice for our beloved children, daughters, sons, nieces, nephew's, grandchildren and, their future generations?

Complete Album Link:

"Satanic Minor Attracted Persons Ped0phile/B LM/ANT◇FA/ LGBTQ Agend

(For some some strange reason although this album is viewable in my album section, the link is broken. If this continues, you can go to my album section and look it up by title.)

◇◇   ◇   Look   at   this   post   on   Facebook https://www.facebook.com/share/soo9f14Nw7fpfEan/?

FULL ◇◇ALBUM:

(WARNING!! E◇TREMELY INTENSE TRUTHFUL CONTENT)

◇ https://m.facebook.com/media/set/?set=a.38717930661164912&type=3&wtsid=rdr_03M6gpTjvDsrFgcM48

I've been waiting for this to finally be acknowledged,...hard to miss;

◇◇ https://www.facebook.com/538690142808571/posts/with-all-that-effort-to-bring-her-inof-which-there-is-a-plethora-of-evidencenow-/3996362857041265

◇Can Anyone Say ◇ Trafficking◇???

"Migrant children "fresh across the border" are riding buses and now flying into Tennessee, sources tell FOX 17 News.

A source close to the situation, speaking on the condition of anonymity to FOX 17 News, gave an inside look at how children are being transported from border facilities into different states. He says a third-party in conjunction with the Department of Homeland Security reached out to him regarding the routes.

"There are drop-offs in small towns and big cities all along the routes. I don't know if they're going into other processing centres. In some cases, family members are waiting to find these children and there have been some emotional reunions. But my understanding in a number of these cases, these kids are fresh across the border. Whether they're going to sponsors, family members, I don't know. They have intentionally not shared a lot of information with us. They don't want this to get out," he said.

According to our source, the Biden Administration has changed their tactics of bringing unaccompanied children into the U.S. and that most of the transports begin in Dallas before sending the children to larger cities like New York, Chicago, or Miami, while dropping kids off to locations like Chattanooga or Nashville along the way.

"They had, to my understanding, a field full of buses with more buses and more buses running all of these routes. Now, they're flying the kids because the buses were easier to videotape going down the highway. They've changed their strategy from buses to flying," he explained. "In Chattanooga and other cities, motor coach companies are waiting on planes to land and continuing their trek further north, dropping kids off along the way."

He says the children being brought Into the country appear to be well-cared for with haircuts and new tennis shoes, but described the hours they spend in transport as sad.

"The bus comes through in the middle of the night. The kids get on a different bus because of DOD regulations. The bus goes another 8 or 9, 10 hours, they'll make a couple stops along the way. I don't know where they're going. Then they'll get on another bus, go another 8 or 9 hours. So they have chained all of these companies together. They go from one bus company to another bus company to another bus company. It's very sad."

Told to stay silent, one bus company's driver bravely spoke to FOX 17 News about traveling with the unaccompanied migrant children. She has been behind the wheel of charter buses for nearly 20 years now and has "never experienced anything like this."

Since the end of April, she has driven three bus loads of migrant children and chaperones with around 30-45 people per trip. She says each of her routes have left her in the dark, with last-minute requests and little to no information other than pick-up and drop-off points.

"I have no idea. I assume they're from Homeland Security, but I have no idea. I myself am kind of in the dark. By the way, I need you here in five hours. Hurry up and pack, here's where we need you. They call me when the first bus leaves. Once I leave, then they're contacting the next driver," she said. "The whole thing is last minute. It makes it easier, it's more protection for the children."

Where are the children from? The driver believes most of the minors are coming from Guatemala, Mexico or Honduras.

"They act like any normal children. They are kind of scared at first because you know they have no idea what's going on. Hardly any of them speak English, so they're scared," she said.

Where are they going? Different locations, but she knows some drop-offs have been in Nashville, Knoxville and Chattanooga.

"I've travelled to several different places. It hasn't always been at the exact same location. There have been some drop-offs in Nashville, some in Knoxville, some in Chattanooga, a couple in Atlanta. That's just as far as I go, then the children continue on further. They're getting dropped off progressively through the whole route," she explains.

With each of her drop-offs, she says chaperones on the bus make sure children are reunited with their parents, relatives or sponsors by checking IDs and passports. She has seen 15 children become reunited with their loved ones so far, with one reunion during her route in Nashville. Choking up, she described the reunions as amazing and heartfelt.

"There is no words to see how happy these children and parents are to be reunited. There's no words," she said. "As a parent myself, I can only imagine what these families go through. To see them reunited is just beyond speech. There's nothing you can say to explain this reuniting of families."

But some say this isn't always the case.

"Some of them are being reunited with family members and that's touching, heart-warming to see, but I think that's the exception, not the rule," one source said.

In response to reports of migrant children entering Tennessee, U.S. Senators Marsha Blackburn (R-Tenn.) and Bill Hagerty (R-Tenn.) sent a letter to President Biden, demanding transparency on the matter.

"There are media reports that, within the last week, at least four planes carrying UACs landed at Wilson Air Centre in Chattanooga, Tennessee, before swiftly boarding the children onto buses and transporting them to multiple cities across the south-eastern United

States for apparent resettlement, with zero transparency regarding what was happening," a representative for Senator Blackburn wrote.

As for Senator Blackburn, she blames the Biden Administration and says she is deeply troubled by the "lack of transparency."

"His administration is secretly transporting the migrants the Border Patrol did catch to communities throughout the United States. They are doing this in the dead of night without the knowledge or permission of the communities involved," Senator Blackburn said. "Joe Biden has put these children at risk. He is putting Tennesseans at risk. The American people deserve the truth now."

Tennessee Governor Bill Lee quickly issued his support for Senators Blackburn and Hagerty speaking out.

"When we demanded answers, they cut off transparency & emboldened one of the worst human trafficking crises we've seen at our border in the last 20 years. I commend Senator Hagerty & Senator Marsha Blackburn for calling this out – Tennesseans deserve to know who is coming into our state," the Governor tweeted alongside a link to a Fox News article.

When asked if the Governor knew of the migrant stops in Chattanooga himself, a spokesperson for Lee said no.

"No, the Biden Administration is not providing any visibility and has not responded to our requests for information. Everything we've learned has been from news reports," the spokesperson said.

Lee previously led a letter to the White House signed by Republican governors across the country telling Biden officials their states do not want to house unaccompanied minors from the border, saying: "We have neither the resources nor the obligation to solve the federal government's problem."

Meanwhile, Immigration Attorney Brittany Faith says many of the unaccompanied minors have been victims of abuse and gang violence.

"I hope the local community will respect their privacy and let them have the space to heal and be reunited with their families," Faith said.

With conflicted opinions on both sides of the aisle, our source believes this is just the beginning.

"They are just getting ramped up. They're just getting started. I can't tell you how many busloads of kids they have already shipped into our country," a source said.

FOX 17 News reached out to the Department of Defence about the migrant children being transported to Tennessee. Eight hours after asking for answers, we have not heard back.

Continued:

◈   https://www.facebook.com/538690142808571/posts/can-anyone-say-traffickingmigrant-children-fresh-across-the-border-are-riding-bu/4941461632531378/

White ◈ Rabbit=Pe do vore ◈ Adrenachrome 'supplies' ◈

"After the Vietnam War, America Flew Planes Full of Babies Back to the U.S.

Operation Babylift had some problems, though.

BY ANDY WRIGHT

SEPTEMBER 21, 2016

The image is common enough: A passenger plane with human cargo belted snugly into their seats. But look for another second and you'll see that every passenger is a child, and each one has been bundled up inside an identical cardboard box. Most of them are babies, but some are older and their limbs spill over the edges of their makeshift bassinets. They appear marooned without any adults in the shot.

The Image is one of many taken during the chaotic end of the Vietnam War when the United States undertook an operation to evacuate thousands of children from Vietnam in April 1975, just weeks before the Fall of Saigon. Supposedly all orphaned, they were slated to be adopted out to waiting U.S. families. Over 2,500 children were brought stateside on flights manned by volunteers outnumbered by infants. Three processing centres were quickly formed at military outposts on the West Coast—two in California and one in

Washington—where children were received before being placed with families throughout the country.

Doubts about some of the children's orphan hood would bubble to the surface almost immediately, but before such questions could even be posed, those tasked with manning the operation had to grapple with an incredible logistical problem: quickly transporting and caring for thousands of infants during a time of pandemonium.

Those who accompanied children on flights—including commercial flight attendants who were recruited or volunteered—used the materials on hand to turn planes into makeshift nurseries.

Flight attendant Jan Wollett told NPR that she and others lined the floor of their plane with blankets for the babies, and secured others with cargo netting.

One Pan Am flight attendant recalled stashing babies in cardboard bassinets both on and underneath seats. During the flight she dodged "midget bodies crawling in the aisles" and checked babies with a flashlight:

"We constantly peeked into bassinets to make sure each baby was still breathing. I froze as I flashed my light on each little back, waiting for what seemed like hours to see a ribcage move with the breath of life."

A nurse who accompanied a planeload of children to Seattle wrote that she was "overwhelmed" as she saw "the endless flow of little ones pouring into the plane filling every available space." She did not sleep during the 30-hour flight.

Jim Trullinger was doing doctoral research in Vietnam when forced to flee the country. He secured a trip back to the United States with Operation Babylift. "When we got to the airport, I helped carry babies onto the plane, a 747 charter, and strap them into their seats," he wrote. "There were no baby carriers, so we just had to use seat belts tightened around the babies. There were so many babies that there was no place for me to sit. Before take-off, the flight attendant told me that if there was a crash, I was to get off the plane first and she would toss babies to me."

Catastrophe was fresh in everyone's minds, as the first scheduled flight of Operation Baby lift flight had crash-landed on April 4th, killing many of the passengers, including 78 children.

Upon arriving in the United States, planes were met by medical teams that triaged groups of children who were suffering from a range of maladies such as severe dehydration, intestinal illnesses, pneumonia, skin infections and even chicken pox. Ambulances rushed the sickest to hospitals. Around half of the children flowed through San Francisco's Presidio. Now a lush recreation area, the Presidio was an army base at the time and a cavernous football field-sized building called Harmon Hall was transformed into a massive care facility.

Michael Howe was the president of the Bay Area Health Planning Council at the time, a voluntary organization that oversaw the direction of healthcare and hospitals in San Francisco. Organizers tapped him to help, and he became a volunteer coordinator at the Presidio, working with nursing students, Vietnam veterans and others to assist in caring for the children. In 2015, Howe revisited Harmon Hall with a group of fellow volunteers as well as men and women who had arrived as children on Operation Baby lift flights. He described the setting as "extraordinary".

"How did we do this?" he wondered, "Did we really do this?"

When the children started arriving, it was a chaotic scene. "There was really no one in charge and in some way it's kind of a misnomer to call me or anybody else a leader—we were there doing what we possibly could do in an environment where we really weren't quite sure what to do, bottom line," says Howe.

The hall was lined with small mattresses for the babies; when mattresses ran short, children were sometimes placed on layers of blankets on the floor. Half of the facility was devoted to support services for the children; part to feeding volunteers who worked long shifts, sometimes sleeping at the facility. The children were sick, and volunteers fell sick as well. In very rare cases, people who felt they had been promised a child for adoption would show up at the Presidio and try to abscond with a baby.

An April 6, 1975 San Francisco Chronicle article reported that there were "7,886 bottles of formula, at least 10,000 disposable diapers, 2,400 cotton tipped swabs and 750 cotton balls, 1,440 aspirin tablets, gallons of baby powder, ointment by the bushel, toothpaste and towels" on hand at the Presidio. The same article described a plane bound for Seattle "crammed with bassinets, diapers, bottles, and food including hot dogs."

As they marshalled the resources to care for thousands of children, volunteers—who were not involved in the decision to receive or adopt out children—quickly began to doubt whether every child was without family

"There are unquestionably children in the airlift who are true orphans," Jane Barton, a translator from the American Friends Services Committee told the San Francisco Chronicle on April 13, 1975. "But I talked to a number of children who said they are not orphans."

Howe, too, had concerns.

"I felt it before we closed out our work," says Howe. "The word 'felt' is important—I had no proof."

Did the U.S. save kids—or steal them? The legacy of Operation Baby lift is a deeply complicated one. Lawsuits were filed on behalf of the children including one brought by the Centre for Constitutional Rights in 1975 that sought to reunite adoptees with living relatives. Some have successfully formed relationships with biological family as adults while others are still searching. Many have made the pilgrimage back to Vietnam to reconnect with their roots, reversing the flights they took over 40 years ago, scattered in the cabin of an airplane filled with crying babies."

Shared with my previous post, this is how they took advantage of Vietnam,...#OperationBabyLift. Follow the white rabbit,...pedovore Adrenachrome "supply" symbol.

Featured Article:

◈◈▶   https://www.facebook.com/5386901428085 71/posts/white-rabbitpe-do-vore-adr-enoch-rome-suppliesafter-the-vietnam-war-america-flew/55054665361 30882/

◈CHILD T R A F F I C KING OPERATION IN PLAIN SITE◈◈!!

◈80,000 CHILDREN DISPLACED DUE TO BERUIT EXPLOSION!! 😈 UNICEF IS DEEP STATE😣◈, PROVIDING PEDOVORES ADRENOCHROME 'SUPPLIES'!!!

◈◈   https://www.facebook.com/5386901428085 71/posts/child-trafficking-operation-in-plain-site-80000-chi-l-dren-displaced-due-to-b-er/4065354046808812/

History is repeatingy itself here.

◈◈◈

OPERATION BABY LIFT IN FULL AFFECT!!

"URGENT VIDEO! OVER 2,000 CHILDREN IN MAUI ARE MISSING...."

◈◈   https://www.facebook.com/1000644993875 93/posts/operation-baby-lift-in-full-affecturgent-video-over-2000-children-in-maui-are-mi/684692517024055/

"WE IN ER, PO D ES TA, MA◈WELL CHILD

A B D U C T I O N COVER-UP, Madeleine McCann Witnesses Described Clinton's Senior Staff and Associates.

Politically explosive Clinton campaign link to international c h I l d po rn ography ring and child a b d u c t I o n of madeleine McCann"

"PO DE STA BROTHERS, ANTHONY WE INER, and JE FFREY EP S T EI N'S GILFRIEND

GH I S LAI NE MAX WELL, all appear to

fit descriptions of suspicious characters provided by Witnesses"

It has always been clear, the Po d esta brothers were clearly seen carrying Mad eleine away. Now, you add W ein er and Maxwell to the mix and, you've got a very familiar pervo cast of characters for a party. The sketches are an exact match.

These images of the Pode sta brothers have been in circulation since Madeleine disappeared, with the Po des tas and, So ros on the island at the same time yet, nothing had ever been done about it, because they are part of the elite paedophile pe do vore child sex trafficking rings around the world.

This Documentary Exposes Buried Case Files on "The Finders" C◇A Cult,...describing the story of six children who were S R A (Sexual R I t u a l Abuse) survivors and, their handlers,... whose incriminating evidence and case were dropped, as a matter of fact, by the C◇A and FB◇,...Revealing historical and widespread practice.

Back in the 80's, Ted Gunderson, Former Head of the FBI, exposed the link connecting the overwhelming paedophile abuse throughout the foster care system, schools and religious organizations. He thoroughly documented and proved all is connected with satanic paedophile rings, lecturing heavily on this subject, amongst many others. He spent many years investigating countless cases, unravelling a web of dark paedophile rings, feeding off our children, on all levels. He slowly deteriorated from Arsenic poisoning, murdered in 2011.

"The children are disappearing in this country, at the rate of 83 per hour, that's over 700,000 children a year". "It is estimated, 2,500 children are kidnapped and murdered, in this country every year. That's an unbelievable figure, yet the FBI refuses to investigate it"

"THE FINDERS" is a C◇A covert operation and, as far as I know, it's still operating. It was established in the early 1960's and, their task at hand was to k I d n a p children....

Continued: https://www.facebook.com/538690142808571/posts/this-documentary-exposes-buried-case-files-on-the-finders-cia-cultdescribing-the/521029016898 1855/

Historic Elite 0CCULT PARTIES FEATURING TABLES LAVISHED WITH GOLD GILDED

"Black Tie, Long Dresses, And Surrealist Heads: Inside The 1972 Rothschild Ball"

"Others have pointed to the disturbing dolls that decorated the tables as a nod to human sacrifice, but there is no evidence to back these claims.

It's no coincidence, however, that actress Marisa Berenson who attended the dinner would later be cast in Stanley Kubrick's Barry Lyndon. Nor is it happenstance that the director filmed his own masked ball at the Rothschild's Mentmore Towers property in Buckinghamshire for his final film Eyes Wide Shut, which contains eerie echoes of the 1972 ball."

https://allthatsinteresting.com/rothschild-party

I've been waiting for this to finally be acknowledged,...hard to miss;

https://www.facebook.com/5386901428085571/posts/with-all-that-effort-to-bring-her-inof-which-there-is-a-plethora-of-evidencenow-/3996362857041265/

They are currently using this bogus N o v id as an excuse to ultimately remove children from families. This is the true motivation behind this agenda,...it always was. They have been pushing to legitimize these actions, as they feverishly lobby to abolish the consensual age of s e x with children,...As the "woke" schools feverishly push the "love is love", "Minor Attracted Person" pe do phi le Trans agenda.

Some comments are downright disturbing,...as pe dov ores are.

While r aping and, torturing these children, they then c u t off their faces, wear them, to further terrorize them,...producing more Adrenachrome,...before completing the sacrifice. They then remove and consume their adrenal gland blood and, body parts.

They are honouring this sick practice, videoed of Hillary Clinton and, Hu ma Abe din, done to a 9 year old girl. The officers who had to view this content were so disturbed, they are still receiving therapy and, most have died since.

DETAILS ON CONNECTED PLAYERS:

"W u h an, S0ros, the Elite and,

Adrenachrome

Adrenachrome has a legal patent that goes way back, infiltrating most supplies that we rely on. What is it and why?

https://m.facebook.com/media/set/?set=a.387179306616491 2&type=3&wtsid=rdr_0uidT8iZkwvuXpy

WTH!! WAYFAIR, "POSSIBILITIES,...WHAT WE DELIVER BY DELIVERING

https://www.facebook.com/5386901 42808571/posts/wth-wayfair-possibilitieswhat-we-deliver-by-deliveringso-i-was-just-hunkering-do/3989823741028510/

Continued:

Ellen D. Has a line of items for sale on Waif Fare under the label, "Bungalow Rose'

Rose is code for ordering a child. Over standing her involvement with pedovore Adrenachrome child trafficking, her sweatshirt is a sick giveaway. Fraz◇zledrip is all about this sick ritual.

https://www.facebook.com/538690142808571/posts/ellen-d-has-a-line-of-items-for-sale-on-waif-fare-under-the-label-bungalow-roser/3996437037033847/

They're caught doing it again now on Etsy!! What?

https://youtu.be/a9ibbXL9HGg?si=6nAPRNX0i4aiZDgt

Another symbolically sick ◇◇skit:

https://youtu.be/7b4bIcllFdY?si=VoC154FIWzU3U1an

"He's EXPOSING the hidden U.S. CHILD C O N C E N T R A T I O N CAMPS used for tra f f I c King | Redacted News"

~ Redacted

Listen, carefully as he is talking in this video correlating to the video shared here I have previously shared a detailed post, shared below, with relation to him discussing the

◇F e d e r a l l y Funded Walmart camps ◇◇where these children are being warehoused and sold off to and for these wealthy clients,..."sponsors".◇

◇ https://www.facebook.com/1000064499387593/posts/listen-carefully-as-he-is-talking-in-this-video-correlating-to-the-video-shared-/750898330403473/

◇"Walmart Missing Children

H um an Trafficking"◇

And The White ◇Vans:

https://www.facebook.com/1000064499387593/posts/each-year-around-800000-children-were-found-missing-in-the-usa-according-to-the-/4952308882636887/

Alphabet/Face, Google, Twitter, Waif Fare, YouTube,...ALL COMPLICIT IN CHILD T R A F FIC KING.

THIS IS WHY THEY'RE FEVERISHLY SHADOW BANNING and, FACTLESSLY CHECKING AWAY THIS VILE TRUTH. BUT, THE FACTS REMAIN.

In Light Of Facebook's Ever Narrowing Censorship,...Now Incorporating Our President,... F AC E BOOK Allowing Child Abuse, and P o r n is NOT OFFENSIVE, HATEFUL AND, HIGHLY ILLEGAL??!

"Facebook could be held 'criminally liable' for encrypted child abuse messages under Five Eyes plans

Five Eyes ministers are concerned that Facebook's encryption plans will put thousands of children at risk of online abuse.

Facebook is to be warned it will be held "criminally responsible" for encrypted child abuse messages, under plans to be discussed by a meeting of the Five Eyes intelligence network of nations chaired by Priti Patel last night.

The Home Ministers from the five - UK, US, Canada, Australia and New Zealand – are understood to have reviewed what action to take following Facebook's refusal to allow the nations' law enforcement agencies "lawful access" to encrypted messages in exceptional circumstances.

The five fear Facebook's plans to extend end-to-end encrypted messages across all its platforms will enable paedophiles to escape detection as they exchange abuse images and permit criminals and terrorists to hide their messages...."

So it's okay to protect vicious paedophiles and, pe do v ores, and, other criminal activity but, we need to be monitored and censored to no avail!?

https://m.facebook.com/
story.php?story_fbid=4013365238674360&id=5386901428085718&mi

The Filthy Wolves in Sheep's Clothing are those we have been conditioned to trust with our most precious and innocent children.

A parent shared this poster from her child's preschool as they were introducing the new, all inclusive sexual education program for their pre-schoolers, with the meaning of,

"LOVE IS LOVE,...NOT AGE"

The Schools Indoctrinating Normalization

"LOVE IS LOVE", NORMALIZING the Terminally
    'WOKE' Agenda of Pan's TRANS-P E D O P H I L I A
    TRANCE Abuse,...Repackaged as,...
    "MAP,... a.k.a., Minor Attracted Person's".

Rising up the TRANS Baphomet through OUR CHILDREN before their brains are formed to think to make a choice for themselves.

◇Research estimates that the BRAIN IS NOT FULLY MATURE UNTIL AT LEAST 30 YEARS OF AGE. This is why 21 was marked for the allowable drinking age. Yet, according to the

Alfred Kinsey's twisted Sado-Pe do sexual education system, beginning at the age of five, children are fully capable of making choices over their bodies, including understanding and experiencing an introduction into adult sexuality,...Particularly that which is against the norm.

"WE'LL CONVERT YOUR C H I L D R E N"

"Democrat led California legislature passes bill reducing penalties for sexual relations with MI NORS"

KUSI News

(Sharing my collaborative post. However, for some strange reason, I'm noticing now on Facebook, my links for my posts are not pasting as viable links. However, if you click this link below, under,.

WAKE UP!!

WHOSE FREEDOM IS THIS FOR

AND WHAT ABOUT??

The True Pandemic,...Changing of Kinds ~ Rising of the Baphomet Machine,...Parents Pushed Aside.

, within this post, you will find the original link which can be clicked on.)

HTTPS://WWW.FACEBOOK.com/100064499387593/posts/the-filthy-wolves-in-sheeps-clothing-are-those-we-have-been-conditioned-to-trust/735000201993286/[1]

"Now she's Entering her Mother of Creation Phase"

Mary/Madonna/Sophia/Lucifer,. Queen of Darkness;

Madonna,... brandishing an unnaturally younger plasticise face ,...

 cheering with "ambrosia" (ad r Enoch Rome) in a wine glass.

---

1. https://www.facebook.com/100064499387593/posts/the-filthy-wolves-in-sheeps-clothing-are-those-we-have-been-conditioned-to-trust/735000201993286/

"In the ancient Greek myths, ambrosia (/æmˈbroʊziə, -ʒə/, Ancient Greek: ἀμβροσία 'immortality'), the food or drink of the Greek gods,[1] is often depicted as conferring longevity or immortality upon whoever consumed it."

"Madonna Investigated for HUMAN

TR A F F I C KING Her OWN Children"

◇   https://www.facebook.com/538690142808571/posts/now-shes-entering-her-mother-of-creation-phase-%EF%B8%8Fmarymadonnasophialuciferqueen-of/6164179070259622/

THE GOAL

"LOVE IS LOVE"

Recent Update (12/2022)

BAAL en c◇a ga and fashions connection with trafficking , fr a zel d r I p and, the White

"Love Is For Everyone,...Someday"

=

"LOVE IS LOVE"

More discussion on suspicious photos and the carefully staged background books, which features horrific bloody occultic images with children

PANDA EYES:

The ad campaign featuring the children with their favorited toys was titled, "Toy Story ". Within that campaign, there was a series called, "Gift Shop", which featured 1 child per ad, surrounded by very disturbing imagery and artwork, as well as the white bunny.

A known symbol for trafficking.

Her runway shows are featuring distressed bruised models, dragging through the dirt, B D S M Teddy Bears, hanging by their neck on a rope? When you look at the gift shop ads with each child featuring an individual B D S M Teddy Bears, bunny rabbit, red face on the wall etc.;...when you understand the symbology, it is clear what each model is holding up for sale. Does Teddy Bears represent a C H I L D f o r s a l e.

Then you have shared video footage of models carrying around B R U I S ED baby dolls, featuring baby gift bags, which include a bloody stuffed animal?

"The BAALen C⬦A Ga Fashion S c andal is So Much WORSE Than You Think"

https://www.facebook.com/100064499387593/posts/love-is-for-everyonesomeday-love-is-%EF%B8%8F%EF%B8%8Flove-from-the-simpsons-show-homer-simpson-/506707718155870/

DIVING DEEPER:

Most successful talent agencies and runway shows are used as blatant advertisement for human trafficking... hidden in plain site .

AUGUST, 2020;

Step hen K ings Blatant Request For Children,...Adrenachrome "Supply"~ Children and mothers for Mars Torture, satanic Sacrifice,...and, B readers...3 Days Ago!!

Two years ago, T rump cryptically stated at a speech that they have PUT A FLAG ON MARS??

Sharing a post on the disturbing images of children in bunny suits (=⬦) in a post that Stephen King put out, requesting children for "Mars", just to make a point Of the code behind with the language is really saying.

Was this what he was speaking about!?!

◇MARS Needs More Moms, More Children??More Information and Updates Shared in The Comments Section of The Main Photo

https://www.facebook.com/538690142808571/posts/step-hen-k-ings-blatant-request-for-childrenadrenochrome-supply-children-and-mot/4059690447375172/

(back up link)

https://m.facebook.com/story.php?story_fbid=4059690447375172&id=538690142808571

MORE CONNECTIONS WITH the actor who played the original Willy Wonka, presenting the Worlds Fair, which actually was one of the worst displays of labelling humanity as a side show and then, resetting history, over and over again.

SHARING MY COLLABORATIVE in-depth posts below. There's a trigger warning here that there are very intense images and content matter being shared, for the sake of education, mentally, physically and, spiritually.

W u h an, S or os, the Elite and, Adrenachrome:

THE RED SHOES CLUB, BLOOD LIBEL

◇https://www.facebook.com/media/set/?set=a.4979421495402058&type=3

"Finders" for The Red Shoes Club:

Ted Gu n de rson, the former head of the F BI, since murdered, exposed the connection of our CPS to 70% of children used in child sex trafficking, Satanic Ri tuals, abuse and, Sacrifice rings. https://www.facebook.com/538690142808571/posts/5937759199568278/?d=n

Regarding the last 10 images with the article, featuring wealthy properties, and their underground tunnels, what is even more eerie, is the 5' high ceilings and rooms specifically designed for children, with relation to Alice and Wonderland programming, used for ritual mind control abuse characteristic of S R A trafficking.

http://www.wsj.com/articles/luxury-homes-tout-underground-tunnels-1433426068

"And It Destroyed Me Because It Destroyed My Illusion of What Rights,...Human Rights Were,...CHILDREN'S RIGHTS WERE. THIS IS A CHILD ABUSE SYSTEM THAT WE HAVE BEEN LIVING IN FOR A VERY LONG TIME AND, ITS BEEN ALLOWED TO GO ON AND,...I WILL NOT BE SILENT ABOUT THIS."

~ john paul rice

Independent producer of, widely the acclaimed film, "A Child's Voice", ..banned from Amazon and other platforms. https://www.facebook.com/groups/483364509289421/posts/9987395446185 79/

Direct testimony link: https://www.facebook.com/1094962718/videos/lets-see-how-long-it-stays-upjohn-paul-rice-independent-hollywood-film-producer-/10222081946653090/

"Because the poor are plundered and the needy groan, I will now arise," says the LORD. "I will protect them from those who malign them." —Psalm 12:5 (NIV)

These are our precious innocent souls, caught up in an evil world, with no consideration or care for the frailty of life.

Sending prayers to our Lord for protection security and, preservation of the innocence of all children around the world.

"Lord, chaos and fear cripple communities overrun by gang violence. Thank You so much for the gift of Your Son. Through Him, we truly become a new creation. We claim Jesus' blessing for peacemakers in Matthew 5:9. Help young people see themselves the way You see them, so they can help bring peace and hope to other people's lives."

"Children are a precious gift from God. As adults, we have the privilege and responsibility to care for them, pray for all children's protection and safety, and help children around us live the full and abundant life God desires for them. Sadly, love and security aren't the reality for hundreds of millions of children who suffer from sexual exploitation, labor in hazardous conditions, or struggle to survive on the streets."

Continued: https://www.facebook.com/100064499387593/posts/because-the-poor-are-plundered-and-the-needy-groan-i-will-now-arise-says-the-lor/686359376857369/

Link to the official page for this info:

https://www.facebook.com/BeatADrumForPeaceALivingMovingCoCreativeTapestry?mibextid=kFx

Then for the people who still can't believe that Adrenachrome is real.

IMARC Group's report, titled "Adrenochrome Manufacturing Plant Project Report 2024: Industry Trends, Plant Setup, Machinery, Raw Materials, Investment Opportunities, Cost and Revenue," provides a complete roadmap for setting up an adrenochrome manufacturing plant. It covers a comprehensive market overview to micro-level information such as unit operations involved, raw material requirements, utility requirements, infrastructure requirements, machinery and technology requirements, manpower requirements, packaging requirements, transportation requirements, etc. The report provides detailed insights into project economics influencing the Adrenachrome manufacturing plant cost, including capital investments, project funding, operating expenses, income and expenditure projections, fixed costs vs. variable costs, direct and indirect costs, expected ROI and net present value (NPV), profit and loss account, financial

Adrenochrome Manufacturing Plant Project Report

Adrenochrome Manufacturing Plant Project Report 2024: Industry Trends, Plant Setup, Machinery, Raw Materials, Investment Opportunities, Cost and Revenue

Report Format: PDF+Excel | Report ID: SR112024A10370

IMARC Group's report, titled "Adrenachrome Manufacturing Plant Project Report 2024: Industry Trends, Plant Setup, Machinery, Raw Materials, Investment Opportunities, Cost and Revenue," provides a complete roadmap for setting up an Adrenachrome manufacturing plant. It covers a comprehensive market overview to micro-level information such as unit operations involved, raw material requirements, utility requirements, infrastructure requirements, machinery and technology requirements, manpower requirements, packaging requirements, transportation requirements, etc. The report provides detailed insights into project economics influencing the Adrenachrome manufacturing plant cost, including capital investments, project funding, operating expenses, income and expenditure projections, fixed costs vs. variable costs, direct and indirect costs, expected ROI and net present value (NPV), profit and loss account, financial analysis, etc.

ADRENACHROME, A NATURALLY occurring compound derived from adrenaline, has captured attention due to its enigmatic associations and controversial reputation. While its precise role in the human body remains a subject of ongoing research, Adrenachrome has garnered interest for its rumored use in various contexts, including conspiracy theories. Though these claims lack scientific backing, the compound's potential effects on cognition and behavior have piqued curiosity. Understanding Adrenachrome necessitates a balanced exploration, separating established scientific knowledge from speculative narratives, shedding light on its actual significance in both physiological and societal contexts.

This compound, despite its controversial reputation, holds potential advantages and applications within the realms of neuroscience and medicine. Research suggests Adrenachrome may play a role in certain oxidative processes that impact brain function, potentially contributing to the understanding of neurological disorders. However, these findings remain preliminary and require further investigation. In the medical field, Adrenachrome potential vasodilator properties have been studied for their application in treating conditions like haemangiomas. It's important to note that Adrenachrome uses are subject to ongoing exploration, and its exact benefits and applications are still a matter of scientific scrutiny, distinguishing concrete findings from speculative claims is essential in assessing its true potential.

The market dynamics surrounding Adrenachrome are influenced by a blend of scientific interest, medical research, and sensationalistic narratives. Although Adrenachrome potential applications are not fully substantiated, its alleged effects on brain function have prompted curiosity among researchers exploring links to neurological disorders. This scientific intrigue acts as a driver, motivating further investigations into its role in cognitive processes. However, it's important to note that the market trends are also influenced by sensational conspiracy theories, which have garnered attention but lack scientific validity. These narratives contribute to the complex landscape around Adrenachrome. As medical research advances, potential therapeutic applications, such as vasodilation for haemangioma treatment, could emerge. Meanwhile, efforts to unravel Adrenachrome true effects and applications from the shadows of speculation remain ongoing, shaping the trajectory of its role in neuroscience and medicine. Given its controversial associations, balanced and evidence-based research is crucial to distinguish valid findings from unfounded claims in driving the understanding and potential market applications of Adrenachrome.

The following aspects have been covered In the Adrenachrome manufacturing plant report:

Market Analysis:

Market Performance

Market Breakup by Segment

Market Breakup by Region

Price Analysis

Impact of COVID-19

Market Outlook

The report provides insights into the landscape of the Adrenachrome industry at the global level. The report also provides a segment-wise and region-wise breakup of the global Adrenachrome industry. Additionally, it also provides the price analysis of feedstock's used in the manufacturing of Adrenachrome, along with the industry profit margins.

Detailed Adrenachrome Manufacturing Plant Process Flow:

Product Overview

Unit Operations Involved

Mass Balance and Raw Material Requirements

Quality Assurance Criteria

Technical Tests

The report also provides detailed information related to the Adrenachrome manufacturing process flow and various unit operations involved in a manufacturing plant. Furthermore, information related to mass balance and raw material requirements has also been provided in the report with a list of necessary quality assurance criteria and technical tests.

Project Details, Requirements and Costs Involved:

Land, Location and Site Development

Plant Layout

Machinery Requirements and Costs

Raw Material Requirements and Costs

Packaging Requirements and Costs

Transportation Requirements and Costs

Utility Requirements and Costs

Human Resource Requirements and Costs

The report provides a detailed location analysis covering insights into the land location, selection criteria, location significance, environmental impact, and expenditure for Adrenachrome manufacturing plant plant setup. Additionally, the report provides information related to plant layout and factors influencing the same. Furthermore, other requirements and expenditures related to machinery, raw materials, packaging, transportation, utilities, and human resources have also been covered in the report

Project Economics:

Capital Investments

Operating Costs

Expenditure Projections

Revenue Projections

Taxation and Depreciation

Profit Projections

Financial Analysis

The report also covers a detailed analysis of the project economics for setting up an Adrenachrome manufacturing plant. This includes the analysis and detailed understanding of capital expenditure (CapEx), operating expenditure (OpEx), income projections, taxation, depreciation, liquidity analysis, profitability analysis, payback period, NPV, uncertainty analysis, and sensitivity analysis. Furthermore, the Adrenachrome manufacturing plant report also provides a detailed analysis of the regulatory procedures and approvals, information related to financial assistance, along with a comprehensive list of certifications required for setting up an Adrenachrome manufacturing plant.

Adrenachrome

Report Coverage Detailed Process Flow: Unit Operations Involved, Quality Assurance Criteria, Technical Tests, Mass Balance, and Raw Material Requirements

Land, Location and Site Development: Selection Criteria and Significance, Location Analysis, Project Planning and Phasing of Development, Environmental Impact, Land Requirement and Costs

Plant Layout: Importance and Essentials, Layout, Factors Influencing Layout

Plant Machinery: Machinery Requirements, Machinery Costs, Machinery Suppliers (Provided on Request)

Raw Materials: Raw Material Requirements, Raw Material Details and Procurement, Raw Material Costs, Raw Material Suppliers (Provided on Request)

Packaging: Packaging Requirements, Packaging Material Details and Procurement, Packaging Costs, Packaging Material Suppliers (Provided on Request)

Other Requirements and Costs: Transportation Requirements and Costs, Utility Requirements and Costs, Energy Requirements and Costs, Water Requirements and Costs, Human Resource Requirements and Costs

Project Economics: Capital Costs, Techno-Economic Parameters, Income Projections, Expenditure Projections, Product Pricing and Margins, Taxation, Depreciation

Financial Analysis: Liquidity Analysis, Profitability Analysis, Payback Period, Net Present Value, Internal Rate of Return, Profit and Loss Account, Uncertainty Analysis, Sensitivity Analysis, Economic Analysis

Other Analysis Covered in The Report: Market Trends and Analysis, Market Segmentation, Market Breakup by Region, Price

Trends, Competitive Landscape, Regulatory Landscape, Strategic Recommendations, Case Study of a Successful Venture

Currency US$ (Data can also be provided in the local currency)

Pricing and Purchase Options Single User License: US$ 3450

Five User License: US$ 4450

Corporate User License: US$ 5450

Customization Scope The report can also be customized based on the requirement of the customer

Post-Sale Analyst Support 10-12 Weeks

Delivery Format PDF and Excel through email (We can also provide the editable version of the report in PPT/Word format on special request)

Take note of the stakeholders and ask yourself now they have a factory but where do they get the supplies?

Adrenachrome is a biomolecule produced in the body by the oxidation of the hormone adrenaline1—hence its name. The "chrome" in its name indicates that it is deeply coloured, compared with white adrenaline.

Adrenachrome was known as long ago as 1856, when French neurologist Alfred Vulpian (who also discovered adrenaline) observed that adrenaline turns red when exposed to air. But it was not until 1937 that David Ezra Green and Derek Richter at the University of Cambridge (UK) named the compound and described its isolation and characterization.

The structure of Adrenachrome Is chiral at the position of the hydroxyl group2. Little information is available on the individual enantiomers. Adrenachrome is an unstable molecule with no practical uses. Its monosemicarbazone (carbazochrome3), however, is stable; it is said to promote blood clotting and can be used to treat haemorrhaging. From the 1950s through the 1970s, Adrenachrome was thought to cause schizophrenia, but this theory was eventually debunked.

In recent years, Adrenachrome has been implicated in far-right conspiracy theories, such as QAnon and Pizzagate reports of satanic ritual abuse, as described in a July 2023 Forbes article. It has also been touted as a hallucinogen or youth drug.

1. CAS Reg. No. 51-43-4; also known as epinephrine.

2. CAS Reg. Nos.: (R)-enantiomer, 7506-92-5; (S)-enantiomer, 5181-82-8.

3. CAS Reg. No. 69-81-8.

Chapter 8 Survivors

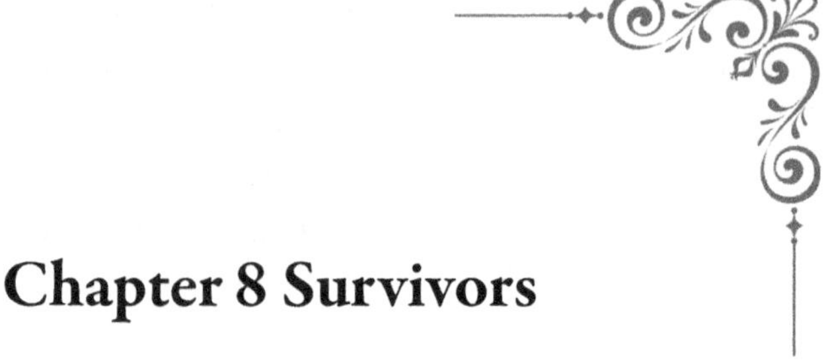

Male
I lived in the same district as Mr. B, who was Well aware that I struggled to feed my family. Mr. B approached me and told me I could Donate a kidney for 1200 Euros. He also Promised me two 'bigah' land in Chitwan. He Said that extracting one kidney would not make A difference to my health. I believed him and in June 2010 we made a long journey to Neighbouring country. We went directly to a Hospital where I was admitted and kept for 15 Days undergoing medical check-ups. On the final Day of my stay they removed my one of my Kidneys and I was immediately sent back to Nepal. I had no idea that having a kidney Extracted in such a manner is a serious crime. After my return my health quickly deteriorated. I Could not work and I was physically as well as Mentally weak. Everything Mr. B had promised Me was not provided apart from a very small Sum of money. In April 2014, I came into contact With the Forum for Protection of People's Rights (PPR) and was provided with counselling and Treatment support by PPR Nepal. After few legal Counselling sessions byPPR's lawyer in my District, a First Incident Report was registered Against Mr. B in accordance with the Human Trafficking and Transportation (Control) Act 2007 which lead to a trial in the district court. In June 2014 the district court ruled that Mr. B Should be imprisoned for three years.

Cristina

My name is Cristina. I am 15 and I come from

Romania. I lived there, and then went to

England. I stayed with my little sisters and brother. I minded them; I was always at home with them. And then... one day, my mother married me off. A friend of hers came to our house and said he wanted to marry me. I heard this, and cried, and did all kinds of things not to marry him. She said: "it's my decision, you just live by it." My husband was 18. I was only 13 and couldn't do anything. He was mean. He didn't know how to act with a girl of 13 or 14. He acted as if I were a woman of 20 or 30. Then I went to Romania where they made my passport and stuff. After that I went to Spain. I stole and he stayed home. I never wanted to steal but I had to or he would hit me. He saw that stealing wasn't working in Spain, so we came to Belgium. I thought what I was doing was wrong and I wanted to stop. I got myself arrested voluntarily. If I hadn't done that, I wouldn't be here. They put me in a centre and I started to live a normal life. When I think about it all my heart breaks.

Many Survivor stories can be found. And some survivors stories was never heard. The effects of trafficking, abduction, illegal adoptions, removal from parental homes and organ harvesting is severe.

Some survivors never recover from the trauma of their past and will have life long psychological damage. Yet the perpetrators are going on with their daily life's.

Brother Nathaniel Skirts Issue of Satanic Ritual Murder
January 26, 2024
Rome had leges, laws, like the Jews. But in their very resemblance lay their difference; for the Roman laws were merely the practical

application of the arma, the arms . . . but without the arms, the leges were empty formulae."

In this extraordinary paragraph, Kastein admits the feeling which the Jewish parasite always feels for the gentile host, "an inhuman hatred". So terrible is this hatred that the most important thing for the Jew is to mask his feelings. Consequently, he always appears bearing an olive branch. His first word is "Shalom or Peace". It is this necessity to conceal his true feelings which leads the Jew to conduct his affairs and his meetings in secret.

JEWS AND RITUAL MURDER.

At the dawn of civilization, the blood rite, in which human blood is drunk from the body of a still-living victim, was known to many tribes.

However, only one people, that has never progressed beyond the Stone Age, has continued to practice the blood rite and ritual murder. This people is the Jews. We have already noted that Arnold Toynbee, a noted scholar, has called the Jews "a fossil people".

In so doing, he must have been aware of the fact that they still practice ritual murder and the drinking of human blood. As a scholar, he could not have failed to note the many attested incidents of this practice of the Jews, for hundreds of examples of ritual murder by the Jews are cited in official Catholic books, in every European literature, and in the court records of all European nations.

It Is the official historian of the Jews, Kastein, in his "History of the Jews", who gives the underlying reason for this barbaric custom. On page 173, he says, "According to the primeval Jewish view, the blood was the seat of the soul."

Thus it was not the heart which was the seat of the soul, according to the stone-age Jews, but the blood itself. They believed that by drinking the blood of a Christian victim who was perfect in every way, they could overcome their physical shortcomings and become as powerful as the intelligent civilized beings among whom they had formed their parasitic communities. Because of this belief, the Jews are known to have practiced drinking blood since they made their first appearance in history.

Civilized people find this practice so abhorrent that they cannot believe it, despite the hundreds of pages of evidence against the Jews which are found in court records. Historical records for five thousand years have provided irrefutable proof of the blood guilt of the Jews. As other people became more civilized, the blood rite became a symbolic one, and a symbolic form of blood, usually wine, was drunk during the ritual, while the barbaric practice of killing a victim was given up altogether. Only one group, the Jewish cult, has continued to practice the blood rite in modern times.

Authorities on the blood rite, such as the noted Catholic scholar, James E. Bulger, state that the Jews practice the blood drinking rite because they are a parasitic people who must partake of the blood of the gentile host if they are to continue to survive. Bulger also states that the drinking of blood is a rite of black magic which enables the Jewish rabbis to predict the future as the blood of their gentile victim courses through their veins. Therefore, Jewish leaders from time to time entice a gentile child, preferably male, and from six to eight years old.

According to Jewish ritual, the gentile child must be perfectly formed, intelligent, and without blemish. He also must be younger than the age of puberty, because the Jews' believe that the blood becomes impure after the beginning of puberty. When the child is enticed into the synagogue, or, if the Jews are under observation, into some more secret gathering-place, the kidnapped child is tied down onto a table, stripped, and its body pierced with sharp ritual knives in the identical places where the nails entered the body of Christ on the cross.

As the blood is drained into cups, the Jewish leaders raise the cups and drink from them, while the Gentile child slowly expires in an atmosphere of unrelieved horror. The Jews call down curses upon Christ and on all the gentiles, and celebrate their symbolic victory over the gentiles as they continue to drink the blood of the dying child. Only by performing this rite, so the Jews believe, can they continue to survive and prosper among the gentile host.

Jews were also feared because of their practice of medicine. In the year 833, the Mohammedans forbade the Jews to adopt the profession of medicine, and in 1335, the Holy Synod of Salamanca declared that Jewish physicians entered this profession solely for the opportunities which it offered them to kill Christians. [This could not be more clear today with mandated Jewish created genocidal VAXX's]

May we continue to waken to the Jewish Plague, for only by recognising the enemy of mankind will we be able to address it.

Mike Stone – Paedophilia is the Power Behind the Deep State
September 1, 2024
"If you've ever wondered why there are so many traitors
On both sides of the political aisle, now you know.
The blackmailers have nearly everyone in public office
In this country by the balls."

By Mike Stone

(henrymakow.com)

What does pedophilia have to do with the current state of the world?

The answer is everything. Paedophilia, child rape, and child sacrifice are the glue that holds the entire Deep State together. Virtually everyone on the Democratic side of the scale is involved, along with a large portion of people on the Republican side. (Check out the allegations against the Bush family and especially against Mike Pence during his time as the Governor of Indiana. You'll be shocked to the core.)

What do you think the Jeffrey Epstein story was all about? It was an Israeli Mossad blackmail operation put together and carried by many of the same people behind the attacks of 9/11.

If you've ever wondered why there are so many traitors on both sides of the political aisle, now you know. The blackmailers have nearly everyone in public office in this country by the balls.

That's not only true in the world of politics, it's also true in big business. Study the Epstein flight logs. How many corporate big shots do you see? How many Hollywood names? If you really want to get to the bottom of it, do some research on Pizzagate. You say Pizzagate was debunked. Not hardly. It was covered up, but never debunked.

Liz Crokin, a Trump confidant, knows the score. She did an expose on Pizzagate, and afterwards ABC News, along with the entirety of the Fake News media, attempted to "debunk" her information. Guess what happened? The reporter for ABC who called it all a "conspiracy theory" failed to discredit a single one of Crokin's allegations, and it turns out that he is a paedophile himself, one who recently pled guilty to child rape. It's the old fox guarding the hen house.

You could say the same thing about the prosecution of the fake Pizzagate "shooter." Guess who the judge was for that case? Kentaji Brown Jackson.

It's not just here either. Paedophilia, child rape, and child sacrifice are taking place all over the globe. The Ukraine was a major hotspot for child trafficking and that's one of the reasons why Russia went in militarily. Look at what's happening in Britain. Judges are letting known pedophiles and child rapists off with a warning, while sentencing patriotic citizens to lengthy prison terms. Why do you think that is?

PROBLEMS AREN'T SOLVED BY IGNORING THEM

You say this is all very interesting. You say that you find child rape, child molestation, and child murder revolting and the bastards doing it should all be locked up. However, there's nothing you can personally do about it.

Actually, there's a lot you can do about it. For starters, you can never vote Democrat again, under any circumstances. To vote Democrat is to knowingly vote for child molesters. That's the reality. And you need to make damn sure you vet anyone running on the Republican side. Many of them are just as guilty. (Note: There is no evidence that Donald Trump or J.D. Vance have engaged in these activities.)

Equally important, you can stop consuming pornography and stop engaging in the mortal sin of masturbation. The people producing and pushing pornography are the same ones behind the rape, molestation and murder of children. And it's not just the porn pushers. It's the entire entertainment industry – music, movies, and television. They're all complicit and if you engage with them on any level, you become complicit yourself.

The truth of the matter is that these people are sick and they are headed straight to the bowels of hell. They hate God. They hate Jesus Christ. They hate humanity. And they lie about everything. You must hold no communion with them whatsoever if you hope to go to Heaven yourself.

Of course, you can take the coward's way out and deny reality. But doing so won't change anything. Reality will remain reality. The only result that comes from denying reality is that it moves you further away from the truth. Now that you know the facts, what are you going to do?

Satanic Depravity Pervades US Government

January 14, 2022

Carolyn Hamlett, a victim of Illuminati paedophilia and brainwashing, responds to Dr. Sue Arrigo's incredible charges that US Presidents and CIA Directors have a lucrative sideline in child sex trafficking and prostitution. She witnessed satanic human sacrifices by top US government officials.

"At the top levels, the FBI, US military and the mob have agreements where they all can benefit. Still a very tricky business, like working with rattle snakes and scorpions. ...On the top levels of the organization, these people are evil and know exactly what they are doing...."

From Aug. 18, 2015

By Carolyn Hamlett

(henrymakow.com)

I grew up in Tampa Florida which was and probably still is one of the worst places in the US for drug and human trafficking as well as being one of the capitals for government sponsored mind control programming.

I know from my own experience that:

1. The child porn industry is real.

I was used in child porn for a period of time. According to what I remember, much of this took place in the basement of Tampa General Hospital in Tampa Florida which was only a couple of miles from my home.

Training children to be sex slaves is real. know exactly what they are doing.

- Children of bloodline families do participate in some of these rituals. Often participation will create a split or more.

5.) Murder of babies and children backed and supported by the US government is real.

I witnessed cold blooded torture and murder of children committed by adults and other children. Most of children used are seen as expendable.

- Some of the torture and murder was done for trauma based programming, some was for entertainment of small groups of well dressed men and women of the "elite".

- I was a victim of both the trauma based torture as well as being the object of torture of social groups who got their jollies out of watching and participating in the torturing and murdering of children.

6.) Child trafficking is real.

- Throughout my childhood I witnessed the coming and going of large numbers of children from MacDill AFB. I also saw children in the belly of ships docked in the ship yard of Port of Tampa that is across the channel from the east side of Davis Islands.

There was a facility that was like a large warehouse or airplane hanger where children were kept in cages. Cages were stacked one on top of another sometimes 3 cages tall. Some cages had one child only and other cages had several children. Throughout my childhood years,

I witnessed the same pattern play out many times. One night there would be a minimum of 3-6 cages with children and the next night there would be 3-6 more. Then the next night there would be so many kids and cages that I could not count them all. Usually the next day they were all gone except for a few. Sometimes the kids were shipped out in 2 separated batches over a two day period.

I don't remember ever seeing no kids at all. There were usually no less than 6 kids. Once in awhile there would only be 3 children, but that was only for a day or so and wasn't the norm.

- Another place where programming and "training" was sometimes done was in a ship docked in the shipyard at the port in Tampa near downtown Tampa. It was on this ship that I have witnessed children being kept.

7.) Government sponsored children facilities where children are kept and used for unethical practices is real.

- I knew of a small facility in Tampa Florida that was near St. Joseph's children's hospital that kept children who were used in horrendous experiments and surgeries. I saw some of the children in that facility. I don't know why I was taken there and shown what I was shown. Maybe it was to send me the message that, that could be my fate also. I do know that the experience left some huge impressions on me other than the horror of what I saw. It was ingrained in me of yet another consequence for those who try to escape and it further instilled in me the message that there is no escape from the perpetrators.

- It was in a wing at St. Joseph's Children's Hospital that a lot of my programming was done. This was also a "teaching" hospital where small groups of adults were being trained to work in the medical field as programmers for the US government. I was used as the subject while my "handlers" demonstrated and taught.

- - It was also at St. Joseph's Children's Hospital that I along with a small group of my preschool friends of a private school on Davis Islands all had our tonsils taken out on the same day by the same doctor and his staff. I remember very clearly what happened to me and some of my friends. This was no ordinary "tonsillectomy". What happened to me was validated by Dr. Preston Bailey Jr. as being typical of an Illuminati procedure employing Illuminati techniques.

- 8.) Training children to be spies and to carry classified information is real.

- - As a very small child I was used often for this because few in those days would suspect that a small child like I would be the carrier of top secret information. I am hesitant to go into detail about this at the moment. I will say this much, that I was a valuable commodity for this type of work for various reasons, one of which was that I was a clairvoyant and was able to "sniff out a rat". The late 1950's, early 1960's was a very dangerous and tricky time in the US military and intelligence. Several factions were at war with each other and were jockeying for control. There was a lot of secrecy within our own military and intelligence. It was extremely hard for one to tell if their best friend was actually their enemy. During that time, I was aware of some very good servants in the military and intelligence who were whole heartedly serving the American public. Those people were dangerous to the the factions who were infiltrating.

- 9.) Facilities with rail access were used in Tampa to hide illegal activities and movement of "goods and services".

- - In the early 1970's I was in two warehouses in the downtown Tampa area that were on the rail and near the Port of Tampa. Both places were involved in trafficking illegal goods. Behind one of the warehouses was a box car that looked like any other normal box car from the outside, but Inside it was equipped with equipment used in mind control programming. This box car was used around the Tampa Bay area as a small portable testing and mind control center that could also transport children to other facilities. The rail car made visits to the University of Tampa and the old Florida State Fairgrounds. Some trauma based programming for children and other young people was done on those grounds.

- 10.) At the top levels, the FBI, US military and the mob have agreements where they all can benefit. Still a very tricky business, like working with rattle snakes and scorpions.

- - In addition to MacDill AFB, Tampa Florida has ports and airports that import and export illegal commodities. I have witnessed the FBI in Tampa taking a blind eye to illegal drug trafficking and moving of stolen goods out of Tampa as long as arrangements have been made to insure that they get a cut of the action in one way or another.

- Related

- By Carolyn Hamlett

SATANIC BLACK MAGIC Rules the World

October 20, 2019

Mankind has succumbed to a broad Luciferian conspiracy. The Epstein affair just scratches the surface. To achieve wealth and fame, ILLUMINATI members must agree to participate in an international CIA-Mossad child trafficking ring. "It's all about blackmail, says Hollywood Insider Isaac Kappy who also claims that Tom Hanks, Steven Spielberg, Stephen King, and Stephen Colbert are pedophiles and Satanists. See also.

Fiona Barnett's testimony that she was an Illuminati child sex slave in Australia is a reminder that while Jews are major players, the Illuminati attracts anyone who is willing to sell his soul for fame and fortune. There are over 300 Luciferian bloodlines and many are not Jewish. "Most of my perpetrators were raised Catholic," she says. While important, the focus on the Jewish role gives non-Jewish Satanists a free pass.

A broad satanic conspiracy has spread throughout the human body politic like cancer.

Makia Freedman writes: "It's a tough and bitter pill to swallow, but we have to face the cold hard truth: the world is run by a Satanic cult, whose members have infiltrated the top layers and power centres of Australian, American and British society (and those of numerous other countries).

Watergate perpetrator, said Watergate solely concerned this human compromise racket, and specifically was an attempt to obtain a list of compromised pedophile VIPs and their proclivities that was held at the Democratic National Headquarters. I spoke with Rothstein who said he knew of an identical VIP pedophile ring that existed here in Australia, and that an Australian intelligence officer named Peter Osborne knew the details of this.

The Australian wing of this child trafficking operation is coordinated by ASIO (Australian Security Intelligence Organisation). During the 1970s and 80s, Labour Party politician, Kim Beazley Sr. headed ASIO's child trafficking operation. Under Kim Beazley's administration, I was prostituted, at age 6 years, to a pedophile orgy at Parliament House in Canberra, where I was raped by then Prime Minister Gough Whitlam, Attorney-General Lionel Murphy, and Governor-General John Kerr. During this same excursion, future Prime Minister Bob Hawke raped me in a suburban backyard near Canberra, and former President Richard Nixon raped me in the back of a US / CIA military plane at Australia's main military airport where Airforce One lands when it visits Australia.

Time, the descendants of these Luciferian pedophile refugees collaborated with existing Luciferian dynasties such as the Kidmans, Conlons, Overtons, Huxleys, Cardens, and Cumpstons, and infiltrated Australian government and influenced law and policy.

This explains why right is being confused with wrong, why the government bodies support the perpetrator instead of the victim of crime, and why our legislation is increasingly reflecting Luciferian pedophile doctrine. This explains, for prime example, why the Australian Human Rights Commission recently defended a pedophile who lied on his job application about his conviction and fined the employee for refusing to hire the pedophile. ... The Jesuits are Luciferians who practice ritual murder and child rape. An increasing number of Australian politicians who hold power are Jesuits.

Owing to his Jesuit training, Leonas Petrauskas assumed the role of head Luciferian priest within the Sutherland Shire Catholic diocese. Roman Catholicism stems from Mithraism, the ancient Luciferian cult in which male priests were married to boy brides (alter boys), and temple prostitutes (nuns) bore children to the priests for ritual murder on key ritual dates. The Latin mass is a whitewashed version of the high Luciferian black mass in which a new-born baby is ritually murdered, and its blood and flesh eaten. This is the ritual that occurred at Bathurst City Hall in 1985, presided over by the AHRC President.

Most of my perpetrators were raised Catholic, and many associated with the Catholic colleges located at Sydney University....

300 LUCIFERIAN BLOODLINES

Luciferianism is arranged according to a hierarchical structure that vaguely resembles a caste system. At the very top sit 13 family dynasties including the Rothschilds and the British Royal Family. These are recognized by the cult as demi-gods. Below these, sit approximately 300 Luciferian bloodlines who are generally high IQ, although this tends to have been watered down in some families due to intermarriage. Below this group sit the commoners who can never attain higher status because they lack the desired bloodline. influence on human behavior. But the impact of indoctrination is reinforced by fear of the consequences of betraying or exposing the cult. The number one rule of Luciferianism is - there is no such thing as Luciferianism. At age of 6 years, I was well taught this lesson. I was taken into a national park. There I witnessed a man (who was a traitor) have each of his 4 limbs tied to 4 different vehicles which drove at high speed in opposite directions. That incident taught me not to talk about the Luciferian cult I was raised in.

Mind control is a Luciferian tradition stemming back thousands of years. Luciferian offspring are trained in witchcraft, astral projection, and psychic manipulation of the physical elements. Children are tested at age 3 for whether they should be raised with conscious or dissociated awareness of their cult involvement. Children with a strong ethical objection to cult practices are never made aware of their involvement.

These children are forced to dissociate through trauma, and their minds fragmented. My husband and I were two such children.

Thanks Debra!

Source

Latest- July 31 Interview with Fiona Barnett

Witness Statement by Fiona Barnett

By Fiona Barrett

(Excerpt by henrymakow.com)

What and Where are MILABS?

By Tory Smith

MILABS are Military Intelligence Laboratories operated by DARPA and the CIA, owned by the Bush family.

There are 39 locations in America with other locations that are connected for child trafficking. The list of operations include #1 The creation of Temporals and AI Drones.

These are used for spying, to commit crimes such as rape and murder. #2

The creation of biological and chemical weapons, including flu viruses and HIV and many others. #3 Child Trafficking.

In the past, Human children were exchanged for weapons and technology. Politicians, Corporate Executives, Military and Police

Officers gang rape and then murder children in service to Lucifer and Satan, who they are required to make a pledge to.

Since the ones who ate the children are gone, now the children are processed into hamburger meat by the Cargill company. #4

Transhumanism experiments. Like the "Borg" in the "Star Trek" series, machine and Humans are combined to make better slaves.

Also Reptilian-Human people are also modified. If you would like to see some of this, look at the artwork of a man named H R Giger. There is also a Netflix Documentary of him. I have witnessed some of the males he has done art work of myself.

The locations of MILABS in America:

Los Angeles #1 and #2, San Bernardino CA, San Jose CA, Carson City NV, Nellis AFB called Las Vegas MILAB, Roswell NM, Albuquerque NM, Denver CO, North Dakota [about 50 mi to Bismark], Lincoln Neb, Minneapolis MN, Chicago #1 and #2, Indianapolis IN, Crawfordsville TX, Dallas, Houston, Jackson Miss, Montgomery AL, Atlanta GA, Grand Rapids MI, Detroit MI, NE Ohio [by Akron near Tallmadge,OH], Pittsburg and Philadelphia PA, Raleigh NC, Langley and Arlington VA, New Jersey [near Newark], 4 in NY- Financial District NYC, Midtown NYC, Montauk, LI, and upstate under a resort community Bolton NY [about 50 mi away], Washington DC #1 and #2, Pentagon, Wilmington DE, and Boston Mass. The locations that are connected for child trafficking are the United Nations Building, the basement of the White House (before President Trump), the NSA spy center in Utah, the TSA location in South Michigan, Orlando FL, Arizona [near Flagstaff] and Seattle.

Other International MILABS are in:

Cern, [close to the Hadron facility] Tokyo Japan, Moscow #1 and #2 [operated by the Russian CIA], Shanghai China, Perth Australia, the Vatican Vatican City Italy, and two in London #2 Essex Road, and London #1 Heathrow Airport, and Dubai. The Vatican and Dubai are almost used exclusively for Temporal creation and child trafficking. The Vatican is used as a distribution center. Mostly refugee children from the USA war crimes, the children are sent to the vatican where they are gang raped, and then are shipped out to over 70 locations in the EU. I became aware of this in January 2013. It took me awhile to calm down and be able to think clearly.

Bush Sr wanted me to join the illuminati and he was the first one to rape me in January 2012. They wanted me because of the gifts Father God gave me, including being able to see DNA of people and read information from it, other psychic gifts and working with various Light energies that God gives us as tools, such as the SACRED FIRE, and the VIOLET FLAME.

The MILAB staff experimented on me for a very long time to exploit my gifts in Healing, including injecting me by needle with HIV 185 times including all 77 mutations, placing snakes and other live animals into my body, such as revealed by artist H R GIGER's artwork, and other horrible activities such as being raped [anal sodomy] by high profile politicians, corporate executives, military males, and police officers.

Also non-human males some of which I can Identify, and some I cannot like this guy... http://cdn.wegotthiscovered.com/wp-co... And a guy like this... http://www.wallpaperup.com/695652/H_R... And a male that looked exactly like this... http://images-cdn.moviepilot.com/imag...

THANK YOU FOR YOUR PRAYERS TO END THIS HORRIBLE TRAGEDY,

Chapter 9 Authors Notes

This was one of the most horrific, heart wrenching studies I ever had to do. I knew some of this existed but never did I think it was so deeply routed and so severe.

During the phase of Investigation I had to take mental breaks in between to calm myself and reflect. As can be seen this is not limited to one specific country but rather a general problem.

The intention of this book is to bring awareness of what is really going on that we don't read in our local news papers. The stories of victims is real.

I can not imagine the suffering some had to endure at the hands of this evil and all for the sake of money.

The exact people who pledged to protect families and children are the ones doing this atrocities. It's a multi billion dollar industry.

To take another human being and torture him or harm him in any way is beyond my comprehension, even more when it's done to vulnerable children.

It's time that we the ordinary citizens wake up from our slumber and say no more. Do what God intended us to do. Protect our children from this evil beings.

My plea is that every person who reads this book, reads it with a open heart and mind. That you will know that this exist and that it will haunt your conscience to action. It's a call to action. Protect your children. Stand up against this tyranny. And say no more. My child, my rules, my way. Intervention into family structures should never be allowed.

Social services was never intended to remove children from their homes, it was meant to assist struggling families. It quickly turned into a money making scandal. And who pays the price for their greed? Our Children! Our families!

It's time we let the governments know to leave our families alone we will raise our children without any intervention. If you see your neighbours abusing their child you intervene and teach the neighbour a lesson. Don't get social services involved, you will be assisting in the total destruction of a child.

Don't miss out!

Visit the website below and you can sign up to receive emails whenever Natashia Roberts publishes a new book. There's no charge and no obligation.

https://books2read.com/r/B-A-LEEBC-CVQAF

BOOKS 2 READ

Connecting independent readers to independent writers.

Also by Natashia Roberts

The Unseen Evil
Hidden Chains

Standalone
Let's Learn Wild Animals
Betrayal And Redemption
A Reise Zu Den Sternen
Once In A Lifetime
Another World
The Unseen Evil

About the Author

Hi my name is Natashia, a mother of 2. I love writing and researching difficult topics. My passion for children made me write books especially for them to help them learn. I hope you find my books helpful.